Keto
Slow Cooker
& One-Pot Meals

OVER 100 SIMPLE & DELICIOUS, LOW-CARB, PALEO AND PRIMAL RECIPES
FOR WEIGHT LOSS AND BETTER HEALTH

Martina Slajerova

FAIR WINDS

Brimming with creative inspiration, how-to projects, and useful information to enrich your everyday life, Quarto Knows is a favorite destination for those pursuing their interests and passions. Visit our site and dig deeper with our books into your area of interest: Quarto Creates, Quarto Cooks, Quarto Homes, Quarto Lives, Quarto Drives, Quarto Explores, Quarto Gifts, or Quarto Kids.

First Published in 2018 by Fair Winds, an imprint of
The Quarto Group,
100 Cummings Center, Suite 265-D, Beverly, MA 01915, USA.
T (978) 282-9590 F (978) 283-2742 QuartoKnows.com

Fair Winds Press titles are also available at discount for retail, wholesale, promotional, and bulk purchase. For details, contact the Special Sales Manager by email at specialsales@quarto.com or by mail at The Quarto Group, Attn: Special Sales Manager, 401 Second Avenue North, Suite 310, Minneapolis, MN 55401, USA.

22 21 20 19 18   1 2 3 4 5

ISBN: 978-1-59233-867-2

Digital edition published in 2018

Library of Congress Cataloging-in-Publication Data

Names: Slajerova, Martina, author.
Title: Keto slow cooker & one-pot meals : 100 simple & delicious low-carb,
   paleo and primal friendly recipes for weight loss and better health /
   Martina Slajerova.
Description: Beverly, MA, USA : Fair Winds Press, [2017] |
Includes index.
Identifiers: LCCN 2017027338 | ISBN 9781592337804 (pbk.)
Subjects: LCSH: Reducing diets. | Electric cooking, Slow. |
Ketogenic diet. |
   Low-carbohydrate diet. | LCGFT: Cookbooks.
Classification: LCC RM222.2 .S5743 2017 | DDC 641.5/884--dc23
LC record available at https://lccn.loc.gov/2017027338

Names: Slajerova, Martina, author.
Title: Keto slow cooker & one-pot meals : 100 simple & delicious low-carb,
   paleo and primal friendly recipes for weight loss and better health /
   Martina Slajerova.
Description: Beverly, MA, USA : Fair Winds Press, [2017] |
Includes index.
Identifiers: LCCN 2017027338 | ISBN 9781592337804 (pbk.)
Subjects: LCSH: Reducing diets. | Electric cooking, Slow. |
Ketogenic diet. |
   Low-carbohydrate diet. | LCGFT: Cookbooks.
Classification: LCC RM222.2 .S5743 2017 | DDC 641.5/884--dc23
LC record available at https://lccn.loc.gov/2017027338

Design and Page Layout: Rita Sowins / Sowins Design
Photography: Martina Slajerova

Printed in China

The information in this book is for educational purposes only. It is not intended to replace the advice of a physician or medical practitioner. Please see your health-care provider before beginning any new health program.

To my fiancé, Nikos, who is my best friend
and the best recipe tester. Thank you for
being able to put up with the everyday
mess in the kitchen!

To my family and friends, especially my
mom and dad, for their endless love
and support. You taught me, challenged me,
and always stood by me.

Finally, I'd like to dedicate this book
to all busy cooks who want to keep their
diet clean and healthy without spending
hours in the kitchen.

Contents

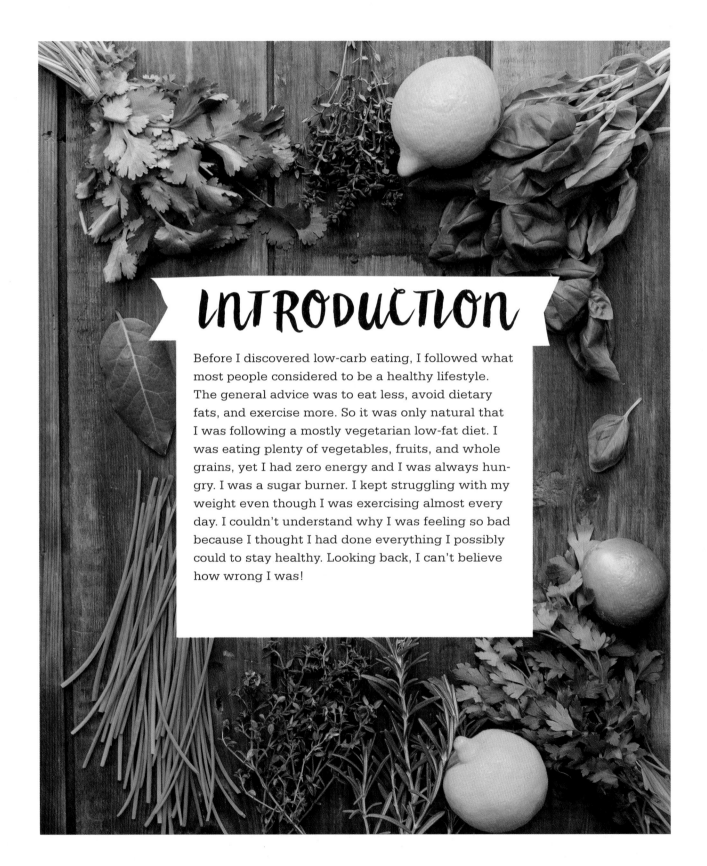

INTRODUCTION

Before I discovered low-carb eating, I followed what most people considered to be a healthy lifestyle. The general advice was to eat less, avoid dietary fats, and exercise more. So it was only natural that I was following a mostly vegetarian low-fat diet. I was eating plenty of vegetables, fruits, and whole grains, yet I had zero energy and I was always hungry. I was a sugar burner. I kept struggling with my weight even though I was exercising almost every day. I couldn't understand why I was feeling so bad because I thought I had done everything I possibly could to stay healthy. Looking back, I can't believe how wrong I was!

What Is the Ketogenic Diet?

The ketogenic diet is a high-fat, moderate-protein, low-carb diet. It's a diet that causes ketones to be produced by the liver, shifting the body's metabolism away from glucose and toward fat utilization. Essentially, your body switches from glucose to fat as the primary fuel. When that happens, it produces molecules known as ketones. (That's where the word *keto* comes from.) The ketogenic diet is not a new concept. It has, in fact, been used for treating epilepsy and other neurological diseases since the 1920s. A well-formulated ketogenic diet can not only help you lose weight, but it can also improve and help treat or manage several health conditions, such as high blood pressure, hormone issues, diabetes, Alzheimer's, Parkinson's, epilepsy, and even cancer.

For me it's not a diet, it's a lifestyle. Studies in *Obesity Reviews* (Santos, et al., 2012) and *New England Journal of Medicine* (Foster, et al., 2003; Samaha, et al., 2003) have shown that low-carb diets outperform other diets in terms of weight loss and health benefits. Unlike other dietary approaches, once you learn the basic principles, it's easy to follow and it's easy to stick with in the long term. You will enjoy the food because fat tastes good and will keep you fuller for longer. I've been following the ketogenic diet for more than five years and I never looked back because I don't ever feel like I am dieting.

A well-formulated ketogenic diet focuses on the amount of carbohydrates *and* on food quality. There is no place for processed foods, artificial sweeteners, and foods laden with unhealthy additives. I rarely buy any packaged foods, especially those with never-ending lists of ingredients and names most people can't even pronounce. A well-formulated ketogenic diet includes healthy low-carb foods, such as non-starchy vegetables, avocados, fatty fish, meat, eggs, and full-fat dairy (if you can tolerate dairy).

Why the Slow Cooker?

Life gets busier and busier. People spend more time at work and less time with their families. Cooking and eating together has become a rare occasion. Eating healthy without spending hours in the kitchen has been challenging for most of us. Don't get me wrong, I love cooking and I enjoy it every time. But I don't expect everyone else to be as enthusiastic as I am, and we all have different priorities. Just like many of you, there are days when I don't have more than fifteen minutes to prepare a meal, and that's when I fire up my slow cooker! I've been using it to prepare healthy keto meals for several years, and it has become a lifesaver.

My aim is to show you that no matter how busy your life gets, you should always find time to eat healthy, even if it means that you don't have more than a few minutes to prepare a meal. Like my *Quick Keto Meals in 30 Minutes or Less* cookbook, this book is full of quick and easy meals that can be cooked by anyone—even a complete novice.

Chapter 1

SLOW COOKING 101

How Does a Slow Cooker Work?

A slow cooker, also known as a Crock-Pot, consists of three main parts: an electric heating element, a cooking dish (stoneware in most cases), and a lid. In a slow cooker, heat is distributed from the bottom and transferred all the way up the stoneware dish. As the food heats up, the steam generated by the heat creates a vacuum seal with the lid.

The slow cooker is an ideal gadget for every busy cook. Food gets cooked very slowly, typically for 4 to 8 hours depending on the temperature setting. Liquids do not evaporate and that's why you can safely keep your slow cooker on all day without supervision. Once your meal is done, most slow cookers switch to a "keep warm" mode so that you can enjoy a warm dinner when you get back from work.

⟶ Benefits of Slow Cooking

TIME SAVER

A slow cooker can provide warming comfort meals and, for those of us who are always busy, it offers the convenience of cooking without all the time-consuming hassle. It can be such a lifesaver when we are short of time and just want to make a big batch of *something* to keep us going throughout the week. You can literally spend just five minutes prepping the ingredients in the morning, throw them in the slow cooker, set the timer, and wait for the magic to happen. When you get home from work, dinner is ready to be served!

MONEY SAVER

Cooking in a slow cooker is budget-friendly for several reasons. First, electric slow cookers are widely available and affordable. The slow cooker also enables you to cook tough, inexpensive meat cuts, such as brisket, chuck, shin, shanks, and oxtails, turning them into hearty stews and wholesome curries. Finally, slow cookers are energy-efficient and waste less energy compared to a traditional oven. It's also likely you will cook meat and sides together instead of having to prepare them separately on the stove or in the oven. It's a win-win!

HEALTHY COOKING

Poaching and braising is by far the healthiest way to prepare foods, especially if you're using the lowest setting on your slow cooker. Low cooking temperatures help retain more vitamins and minerals. Plus, tough meat cuts contain the largest amount of connective tissue high in collagen and elastin. Collagen is transformed into gelatin by cooking. It has several benefits:

- It can keep your joints, ligaments, tendons, and bones healthy, and it can reduce joint pain.
- It's good for your gut and helps with intestinal permeability, a.k.a. "leaky gut."
- It's great for thyroid health and helps fight adrenal fatigue. Collagen is especially great for women with thyroid issues.

Step-by-Step Guide to Slow Cooking

PREPARE THE INGREDIENTS

Preheat the slow cooker while you prepare the ingredients. Most slow cooker recipes require basic prep work, such as slicing the vegetables and adding everything to the slow cooker. Browning and searing the meat and vegetables before slow cooking them is optional, but it will enhance the flavor of your dish.

WHEN COOKING IN A SLOW COOKER, THE ORDER MATTERS

1. Start by layering the firm vegetables, such as rutabaga and turnip, on the bottom.
2. Top with meat. You can use a large variety of meats, such as beef brisket, short ribs, chuck, pork shoulder, and lamb leg or shanks. Apart from tough meat cuts, you can use ground meat, chicken, fish, and seafood.
3. Add aromatics, such as onion, garlic, lemon juice, chiles, ginger, celery, and peppers, and add liquid ingredients, such as tomato puree, bone broth, or stock.
4. Add herbs and spices, such as paprika, cumin, chili powder, cinnamon, coriander, basil, oregano, thyme, rosemary, or parsley. Herbs will lose their flavor after prolonged cooking, and it's good to add some more near the end of the cooking process.

5. Some vegetables may overcook and become mushy. If using medium-tender vegetables, such as broccoli and cauliflower, add them in the last 2 to 4 hours of the cooking process. If using soft vegetables, such as zucchini or chard, add them to the slow cooker near the end of the cooking process, during the last 1 to 2 hours.

6. Add dairy, such as cream, cheese, sour cream, and cream cheese, and coconut milk and cream, at the end of the cooking process, in the last 15 to 30 minutes. Prolonged cooking may result in the sauce breaking.

AVOID COMMON MISTAKES

Do

- Preheat the slow cooker. If you start with a cold slow cooker, you will need to add an extra 15 to 20 minutes to your cooking time.

- Use the right temperature setting. Typically, there are two temperature settings. The rule of thumb is to cook tender meats, such as chicken and fish, on a low temperature setting for 2 to 6 hours (depending on type and size). Cook tough meat cuts, such as brisket and shoulder, on low for 6 to 8 hours or on high for 3 to 4 hours (in some cases even longer). *Warning:* Not all slow cookers are equal. After trying three different brands, I realized that the temperature settings were not the same across all three of them. It may take some trial and error to get the temperature setting right, especially when making delicate recipes like cakes.

- If you are cooking a large meat cut that is more than 3 pounds (1.4 kg), cut it in half to ensure even cooking.

- If you are busy in the morning, prepare everything the night before, place it in the slow cooker dish, cover, and store in the fridge. When you wake up, take it out from the fridge and leave it on the kitchen counter for 15 to 20 minutes. This will allow the ingredients to come closer to room temperature before cooking in the slow cooker.

- Use a thermometer to check when your meat is cooked, especially if you cook large cuts of meat.

- If cooking tough meat cuts that require 6 to 8 hours of cooking, add most vegetables in the last 2 to 4 hours of the cooking process. Also, avoid cutting vegetables too small or they will overcook.

- Keep your food safe. Don't leave the food in the slow cooker once it's cooked. Let it cool down, place in airtight containers, and refrigerate or freeze. Most slow cookers will automatically switch to a "keep warm" mode that will keep the dish warm for a few more hours without spoiling, but it may overcook the dish if used for too long.

- Are you short on time? Simplify the preparation process! You can skip browning the vegetables and meat. Although browning is great for boosting the flavor, it is not essential in most recipes. Just throw all the ingredients in a slow cooker and let it do its job.

- Do you have leftover juices from last night's roasts? Use them to cook your vegetables to boost flavor and nothing goes to waste.

- Use leftover bones and cartilage to make homemade stock (page 28) or broth (page 44). Place them in a freezer bag and make a batch when you collect enough bones.

- Buy cheap meat cuts. The beauty of having a slow cooker is that you can transform inexpensive meat cuts, such as chuck and brisket, into delectable meals.

- Foods cooked at high altitudes take longer to cook. If you live at high altitude, add an additional 1 hour for every 2 hours of cooking.

- If converting your favorite recipe for the slow cooker, be sure to pick the right recipe. Most soups, stews, and casseroles are guaranteed to work. Pay extra attention if converting a dessert (see page 12 for more tips).

Don't

- Do not underfill or overfill your slow cooker. Ideally, your slow cooker should be at least half full and no more than three-quarters full.

- Do not use frozen meat and vegetables. They slow down the cooking process and create an ideal environment for bacteria to thrive.

- Go easy on the liquids. Slow cookers have very little to no evaporation. If you're adapting a stove-top recipe, you will need to reduce the amount of liquids. You can always add more water or liquids near the end of the cooking process if the sauce is too thick. Some recipes, such as Beef Short Ribs (page 141), will only need ¼ cup (60 ml) of water. Using too much water will, in fact, draw more moisture from meat and will dry it out. Desserts and sweet treats need extra attention. It's easy to get the liquids wrong, and your cake will be too moist or too dry.

- When the cooking is in progress, do not open the lid unless you need to add more ingredients (e.g., large roasts will need longer to cook compared to tender vegetables). If you do have to remove the lid (and in some cases you will need to), add 20 to 30 minutes to the cooking time.

- Do not use whole nuts when making a dessert that includes liquids. Whole nuts will soak up all the liquids and will become unpalatable. Recipes with little to no liquids, such as Spiced Macadamia Nuts (page 187), are fine.

- Don't touch the outside casing of the slow cooker when it's in process. It becomes very hot and you should only touch it with oven mitts. For the same reason, be sure to keep your cooker away from curtains, walls, and any other flammable items.

- Don't place the hot ceramic bowl directly on your kitchen counter. Always place it on a cooling rack.

MAKING DESSERTS IN A SLOW COOKER

Desserts Are Best Cooked on "Low"

Delicate recipes, such as cakes and custards, are best prepared on low. Using the high temperature setting may result in uneven cooking and in some cases burned cakes, especially if you use nut flour and a smaller amount of liquids.

Turn the Bowl Halfway Through

Not all slow cookers cook evenly. To prevent uneven cooking or even burning, simply turn the bowl 180 degrees halfway through the cooking process to ensure even cooking. This is important if you're making a recipe with very little liquid, such as Chocolate Chip Cookie Bites (page 188).

Parchment Paper for Easy Manipulation and Reduced Condensation

Some recipes call for a heavy-duty parchment paper that helps in three different ways. First, it will be easier to remove the cooked product from the slow cooker. Secondly, it reduces the risk of burning and sticking to the bowl. Lastly, it helps reduce moisture from excess condensation, because most of the condensation is dripping down the sides in between the food and the bowl. In my experience, if you're using a heavy-duty parchment paper with an aluminum layer, you won't need to use the method below to reduce the condensation.

Paper Towel for Reduced Condensation

There is very little loss of liquids in slow cooker meals, and some recipes require special treatment, especially desserts and some savory recipes. To avoid condensation and water dripping down the sides of the cooker and back onto the dish, place two layers of high-absorbent paper towel or a tea towel on top of the ceramic bowl, cover with a lid, and cook according to recipe instructions. While this is not needed in some recipes (such as Carrot Cake Oatmeal, page 178), it improves the texture of recipes where water drips down the sides directly into the dish and you don't use heavy-duty parchment paper to isolate the dish from the moisture (see "Apple" Pie Crumble, page 180).

DIY Spacer

Some recipes, such as the Snickerdoodle Crème Brûlée (page 181), require a gentle cooking technique using a bain-marie (see page 13). In order to cook the custard evenly, the ramekins should not touch the ceramic bowl. You can either use a grid that is sometimes provided with a slow cooker, or make your own spacer. Simply squeeze a long piece or aluminum foil into a donut shape and press the ends together to close into a circle. Each spacer should hold one ramekin.

Bain-marie

Some recipes, especially deserts, will require a gentle cooking technique called bain-marie, also known as water bath. To speed up the cooking process, always use boiling water for your bain-marie and pour it into the slow cooker before adding the ramekins to avoid accidental spillage into your dish.

Cut Your Cake Like a Pro

When making a cake directly in the slow cooker, you will end up with a rather unusual shape, which is best cut into 13 or 20 pieces. See page 193 for an example of how to cut your cake.

OTHER COOKING METHODS

Slow Cookers versus Dutch Ovens

This is my slow cooking routine in most cases: First, I brown the meat and aromatics in the Dutch oven. Then I transfer both to the slow cooker together with spices, herbs, and liquids. Then I add vegetables (usually in the last 2 to 4 hours of the cooking process). Sometimes, after it's cooked, I crisp up the finished dish in the oven for a few minutes.

Although I love the convenience of browning vegetables and meat, and then cooking in the same pot, I prefer using a Dutch oven first and using the slow cooker afterward. Unlike a Dutch oven, it's safe to leave your slow cooker on even when you're not at home.

Tips for Pressure Cookers and Instant Pots

- Just like slow cookers, pressure cookers are ideal for making flavor-packed soups and stews, and turning inexpensive meat cuts into wholesome dishes. In general, almost every soup and stew that is suitable for a slow cooker can also be made in a pressure cooker.

- Although there is little evaporation with a slow cooker, you will need to use at least 1 cup (240 ml) or more of water when using a pressure cooker.

- If you use ingredients that require different cooking times, you can add them in phases just as you would with a slow cooker. The only inconvenience is that you will have to wait for the pressure to release and build up again.

- Thickeners (see page 29) and dairy should not be used when cooking in a pressure cooker. They should be added afterward.

- Cooking times are cut down dramatically when using a pressure cooker. If a slow cooker recipe takes 4 hours on high or 8 hours on low, it will need between 30 and 40 minutes in the pressure cooker (plus building up and releasing pressure, which will take another 30 to 40 minutes). The exact time depends on the size of the cut, and it can range between 10 minutes and 1 hour. You can find all times required for different meat cuts at instantpot.com/cooking-time.

⟶ Healthy Keto Cooking

COOK WITH HEALTHY FATS

You should pay extra attention to fats because most of your calories should come from them. Unhealthy fats can do as much damage as excessive carbohydrates.

Healthy Cooking Fats

Use oils and fats high in saturated fats (SFA), such as pastured lard, grass-fed beef tallow, chicken fat, duck fat, goose fat, clarified butter or ghee, butter, virgin coconut oil, and sustainably sourced palm kernel oil.

Fats Suitable for Light Cooking and Cold Use

Oils high in monounsaturated fats (MUFA), such as extra-virgin olive oil, avocado oil, and macadamia nut oil, are best for cold use, stir-fries, finishing meals, or after cooking.

Fats Only Suitable for Cold Use

Oils high in polyunsaturated fats (PUFA) are only suitable for cold use, such as in salad dressings and mayonnaise (page 25). These include nut and seed oils such as walnut, almond, hazelnut, flaxseed, sesame seed, or pumpkin seed oil. When you use oils high in omega-6 fatty acids, increase your intake of omega-3 fatty acids, especially from animal sources.

Always Avoid

Not all fats are suitable for a healthy, low-carb diet and, unfortunately, the most commonly used oils are unhealthy. All of the following options should be avoided: vegetable oils and shortening; hydrogenated and partially hydrogenated oils; margarine; and sunflower, canola, safflower, soy, cottonseed, or grapeseed oil. They are highly processed, inflammatory, and prone to oxidation.

What Does Eating "ad libitum" Mean?

When following a ketogenic diet, you should be eating to satiety (ad libitum). Aim for an adequate protein intake (see page 16) and use fat as a "filler" to sate your appetite while keeping carbs low, at 20 to 30 grams of net carbs. It's true that most people following the ketogenic diet don't need to count calories because they don't feel hungry and overeating is unlikely. The ketogenic diet is about getting the right amount of protein and fat to suit your individual needs: some people may be doing well on a diet with 60 percent of calories from fat while others may do better with a higher fat intake (typically during weight maintenance). Keep in mind that what matters is not relative percentages but grams of fat and protein per day. If you want to find out your ideal calorie intake, visit my blog at ketodietapp.com/blog/page/KetoDiet-Buddy.

CHOOSE YOUR PROTEINS WISELY

Just like fats, proteins play an important role in a healthy keto diet. Always buy the best quality of protein sources you can afford.

Meat & Eggs

When it comes to meat, quality matters. If your budget allows it, opt for organic eggs and grass-fed, humanely raised meat. Grass-fed beef contains more micronutrients and more omega-3 fatty acids. Additionally, pasture-raised and grass-fed animals have a much better quality of life compared to those kept in large industrial facilities. There is no need to splurge on expensive meat cuts to get quality tender meat. Opt for the "less desirable" beef brisket, chuck roast, pork shoulder, or lamb shanks.

Warning: When using raw eggs (Quick Mayonnaise, page 25), you should use only fresh, clean, properly refrigerated grade A or AA eggs with intact shells due to the slight risk of salmonella and other foodborne illnesses. Avoid contact between the yolks or whites and the outside of the shell. Prevent any risks by using eggs with pasteurized shells.

To pasteurize eggs at home, simply pour enough water in a saucepan to cover the eggs. Heat to about 140°F (60°C). Using a spoon, slowly place the eggs in the saucepan. Keep the eggs in the water for about 3 minutes. This should be enough to pasteurize the eggs and kill any potential bacteria. Let the eggs cool down and store in the fridge for 6 to 8 weeks.

Fish & Seafood

Avoid farmed fish and opt for wild-caught, locally sourced, sustainable fish. Imported farmed fish are exposed to antibiotics and chemicals, and they are often stored in bacteria-laden ice. Many species of fish have become overfished due to destructive harvesting methods that have a direct effect on the marine life.

And it doesn't end there. Our oceans are polluted and mercury levels in fish are higher than ever. Mercury is known to accumulate in fish and is dangerous to humans, especially pregnant women and young children, because it can damage the central nervous system. As a general rule, large fish that are higher up in the food chain are more likely to contain higher levels of mercury. The smaller the fish, the lower the mercury levels.

So what's your best choice? Some of the best options according to the Seafood Watch Best Choices list are: Pacific sardines, Atlantic mackerel, freshwater Coho salmon, Alaskan salmon, canned salmon, Albacore tuna, and sablefish/black cod. All of the above are low in mercury and good sources of omega-3 fatty acids. To learn more about sustainable fish low in mercury, visit seafoodwatch.org and get the free Seafood Watch app.

What is Adequate Protein Intake?

According to Jeff Volek, Ph.D., R.D., and Stephen Phinney, M.D., Ph.D., best-selling authors of *The Art and Science of Low Carbohydrate Performance*, you will need between 0.6 and 1 gram per pound (1.3 to 2.2 grams per kilogram) of lean mass. In most cases, this translates to 65 to 80 grams of protein per day, sometimes even more. The exact amount depends on gender, lean mass weight, and activity level.

Don't get obsessed over your protein intake. Eating slightly more protein will not kick you out of ketosis or impair your progress. Studies in the *American Physiological Society* (Jahoor, et al., 1990) and *The Journal of Clinical Endocrinology & Metabolism* (Bisschop, et al., 2000) have shown that you would have to be eating huge amounts of protein to go into gluconeogenesis (converting protein to glucose). Remember, protein is the most sating macronutrient; it will help you feel less hungry and eat fewer calories. When you eat a high-protein meal, you body releases glucagon, which counterbalances insulin and plays a significant role in satiety. That's why it's imperative to eat adequate amount of protein if your aim is to lose body fat.

This doesn't mean that you should overeat protein. Protein is not a particularly efficient fuel source and too much of it may raise your insulin levels. If you are insulin resistant or diabetic, be aware that not all protein sources are equal and some, such as whey protein, will cause greater insulin responses than others. Also, those who suffer from diabetic nephropathy, a type of kidney disease caused by diabetes, will need to eat less protein.

CARBOHYDRATES ON THE KETOGENIC DIET

When following a ketogenic diet, you should aim for no more than 50 grams of total carbohydrates (20 to 30 grams of net carbohydrates) per day, mostly from non-starchy vegetables, avocados, and nuts. Everyone tolerates a slightly different carbohydrate level, and you'll need to try and find out what works best for you.

The suggestion that the "zero-carb" approach leads to a higher level of ketones and enhanced fat loss is misleading because this is not the main reason for weight loss on the ketogenic diet. It's simple: you will eat less because the ketogenic diet has natural appetite-suppressing effects. There is no scientific evidence that high levels of ketones will lead to enhanced fat loss. Typically, a zero or very low-carb approach may be desirable purely for therapeutic purposes rather than fat loss.

Total Carbs or Net Carbs?

Net carbohydrates are total carbohydrates without fiber. There are two types of fiber: soluble and insoluble. While soluble fiber contains calories, insoluble fiber has zero calories and zero effect on blood sugar. Most foods contain both types of fiber, and foods eaten on a ketogenic diet tend to be higher in insoluble fiber (avocados, nuts, leafy greens, etc.). Fiber has little to no effect on blood sugar, and counting net carbs works well for most people seeking to lose weight and those who want to improve their overall health. However, counting total carbs may be a better option for managing a disease, such as cancer, epilepsy, or Alzheimer's, where carbohydrate restriction is more severe.

Although I follow what is known as the "net carb approach," you can use my book even if you use the total carb approach. All of my recipes include a detailed nutritional breakdown, listing both total and net carbs.

SWAP LOW-CARB VEGETABLES FOR STARCHY SIDES

Zucchini Noodles

Use a julienne peeler or a spiralizer to turn the zucchini into thin or wide "noodles." Chop the soft cores and add them to the noodles. Sprinkle the noodles with salt and let them sit for 10 minutes. Use a paper towel to pat them dry. Set aside.

RECOMMENDED SERVING SIZE: 1 small (150 g/5.3 oz) to medium (200 g/7.1 oz) zucchini
CARBS PER 1 SMALL ZUCCHINI: 3.2 g net carbs, 4.7 g total carbs
CARBS PER 1 MEDIUM ZUCCHINI: 4.2 g net carbs, 6.2 g total carbs

Cauli-rice

Wash the cauliflower thoroughly and drain well. Once dry, grate with a hand grater, or place the florets in a food processor with a grating blade and pulse until it looks like rice. A grating blade will make it look closer to real rice. Don't overdo it. It only takes a few more seconds to make purée out of your cauliflower. Place in an airtight container and store for up to 4 days.

Cook your cauli-rice using these methods:

Steaming: Place in a steam pot and cook for 5 to 7 minutes.

Microwaving: Place the processed cauliflower in a microwave-safe bowl and cook on medium-high for 5 to 7 minutes. You won't need any water when cooking in the microwave.

Pan roasting: You can briefly cook the cauli-rice on a pan greased with butter or ghee, or add it directly to the pot with meat or sauce you plan to serve it with. This method adds extra flavor to your cauli-rice!

Oven cooking: Preheat the oven to 400°F (200°C, or gas mark 6). Spread the grated cauli-rice on a baking sheet lined with parchment paper and cook for 12 to 15 minutes, flipping two or three times. This method is great when you want the rice to be as dry as possible.

RECOMMENDED SERVING SIZE: 1 to 1½ cups (120 to 180 g/4.2 to 6.4 oz)
CARBS PER 1 CUP (120 G): 3.6 g net carbs, 6 g total carbs
CARBS PER 1½ CUPS (180 G): 5.4 g net carbs, 9 g total carbs

Shirataki Noodles/Rice

Wash the shirataki noodles thoroughly and boil them for 2 to 3 minutes. Drain well. Place the noodles in a hot dry pan. Fry over medium-high heat for about 10 minutes. Using tongs, toss the noodles as they cook. Add the fried noodles directly to a meal, or place in an airtight container and refrigerate for up to 3 days.

RECOMMENDED SERVING SIZE: 3.5 to 5.3 oz (100 to 150 g)
CARBS PER 3.5 OZ (100 G): 1.5 g net carbs, 2.9 g total carbs
CARBS PER 5.3 OZ (150 G): 2.3 g net carbs, 4.4 g total carbs

Spaghetti Squash

Preheat the slow cooker and fill with ½ cup (120 ml) of water. Prick the spaghetti squash several times so that the steam can escape while cooking. Place in the slow cooker and cook on low for 4 hours for average-sized squash, or up to 6 hours for large. When done, remove the squash from the slow cooker. Leave it to cool on a cutting board for 20 minutes, then cut it in half lengthwise or widthwise (this will result in longer strands). Spoon out the seeds and discard. Using a fork, pull the strands out and place them in a bowl.

Cooked spaghetti squash can be stored in the fridge in an airtight container for up to 5 days. For longer storage, divide it into manageable portions and place it in plastic bags, flatten, and freeze flat. The frozen squash will keep for up to 6 months. When ready to serve, let the prepared squash defrost at room temperature or in the fridge.

RECOMMENDED SERVING SIZE: ¾ to 1 cup (116 to 155 g/4.1 to 5.5 oz) cooked spaghetti squash
CARBS PER ¾ CUP (116 G): 5.8 g net carbs, 7.5 g total carbs
CARBS PER 1 CUP (155 G): 7.8 g net carbs, 10 g total carbs

When Should You Buy Organic?

Not all fruits and vegetables need to be labeled organic to be safe to eat. So which ones are worth paying for? Simple! If it's on the Dirty Dozen list (www.ewg.org), always buy organic.

OVERVIEW OF LOW-CARB VEGETABLES

Here are some more healthy veggies that you can use as sides (avocados are technically a fruit, but are included here as they're a staple of the keto diet). All information is per raw vegetables.

FOOD	SERVING SIZE	TOTAL CARBS (G)	NET CARBS (G)
Arugula	2 cups (20 g/0.7 oz)	0.7	0.4
Asparagus	1 small bunch (150 g/5.3 oz)	5.8	2.7
Avocado	medium-size (150 g/5.3 oz)	12.8	2.7
Bean sprouts	1 cup (50 g/1.8 oz)	3.0	2.0
Broccoli, raw, chopped	1½ cups (137 g/4.8 oz)	9.1	5.5
Brussels sprouts, halved	1¼ cups (110 g/3.9 oz)	9.8	5.7
Cabbage, green, chopped	1½ cups (135 g/4.8 oz)	7.7	4.3
Cabbage, red, chopped	1½ cups (135 g/4.8 oz)	9.9	7.1
Cabbage, white, chopped	1½ cups (135 g/4.8 oz)	7.7	4.4
Cauliflower, chopped	1½ cups (161 g/5.7 oz)	8.0	4.8
Celery stalk	2 large (128 g/4.5 oz)	3.8	1.8
Celeriac (celery root), diced	½ cup (78 g/2.8 oz)	7.2	5.8
Cucumber	1 small (150 g/5.3 oz)	3.2	2.2
Endive	1 small (150 g/5.3 oz)	5.0	0.4
Eggplant	½ medium (150 g/5.3 oz)	8.8	4.3
Fennel, sliced	1½ cups (131 g/4.6 oz)	9.5	5.5
Kale, curly	2 cups (100 g/3.5 oz)	5.6	3.6
Kale, dark cavolo nero	2 cups (100 g/3.5 oz)	4.5	1.4
Kohlrabi, diced	1 cup (135 g/4.8 oz)	8.4	3.5
Lettuce, iceberg, shredded	2 cups (144 g/5.1 oz)	4.3	2.5
Lettuce, Little Gem, shredded	2 cups (144 g/5.1 oz)	3.6	2.2
Lettuce, radicchio, shredded	3 cups (120 g/4.2 oz)	5.4	4.3
Lettuce, romaine, shredded	3 cups (141 g/5 oz)	4.6	1.7
Okra, chopped	1 cup (100 g/3.5 oz)	7.5	4.3
Radishes, sliced	1 cup (116 g/4.1 oz)	3.9	2.1
Rutabaga	¾ cup (105 g/3.7 oz)	9.1	6.6
Spinach	4 cups (120 g/4.2 oz)	4.4	1.7
Swiss chard, chopped	4 cups (144/5.1 oz)	5.4	3.1
Tomatoes	1 medium (123 g/4.3 oz)	4.8	3.2
Turnips, diced	1 cup (130 g/4.6 oz)	8.4	6.0
Watercress, chopped	3 cups (102 g/3.6 oz)	1.3	0.8
Zucchini, chopped	1½ cups (186 g/6.6 oz)	5.8	3.9

HERBS AND SPICES ARE YOUR FRIENDS

Herbs and spices will boost flavor while keeping your carbs low. Here are some simple DIY spice blends and curry pastes that will make your keto cooking tasty and effortless.

Cajun Seasoning:

To make about $^2/_3$ cup (95 g) of Cajun seasoning, mix 4 tablespoons (28 g/1 oz) paprika, 2 tablespoons (20 g/0.7 oz) garlic powder, 2 tablespoons (14 g/0.5 oz) onion powder, 2 tablespoons (11 g/0.4 oz) dried oregano, 2 tablespoons (9 g/0.3 oz) dried thyme, 1 tablespoon (7 g/0.3 oz) ground black pepper, and 2 teaspoons cayenne pepper. You can optionally add 1 tablespoon (17 g/0.6 oz) salt or skip and add it directly to the dish. Store in an airtight container for up to 6 months.

Ranch Seasoning:

To make about $^2/_3$ cup (65 g) of ranch seasoning, mix 3 tablespoons (5 g/0.2 oz) dried parsley, 2 tablespoons (4 g/0.2 oz) dried chives, 2 tablespoons (20 g/0.7 oz) garlic powder, 2 tablespoons (14 g/0.5 oz) onion powder, 1 tablespoon (3 g/0.1 oz) dried dill, 1 tablespoon (17 g/0.6 oz) fine sea salt, 1½ teaspoons ground black pepper, and ¾ teaspoon cayenne pepper. Store in an airtight container for up to 6 months.

Pumpkin Pie Spice:

To make about ½ cup (50 g) of pumpkin pie spice, mix 4 tablespoons (31 g/1.1 oz) cinnamon, 2 tablespoons (10 g/0.4 oz) ground ginger, 2 teaspoons ground nutmeg, 1 teaspoon ground cloves, and 1 teaspoon ground allspice. Optionally, add ½ teaspoon ground cardamom and ½ teaspoon ground mace. Store in an airtight container for up to 6 months.

Indian Curry Paste Three Ways

Tikka Masala Curry Paste:

4 cloves garlic, peeled
1 small (14 g/0.5 oz) red chile pepper,
    halved
2½-inch piece (15 g/0.5 oz) ginger
    root, peeled
1 tablespoon (6 g/0.2 oz) garam
    masala
1 tablespoon (6 g/0.2 oz) paprika
2 teaspoons ground cumin
2 teaspoons ground coriander
1 teaspoon turmeric powder
½ to 1 teaspoon cayenne pepper
1 teaspoon fine sea salt
1 bunch (30 g/1.1 oz) fresh cilantro,
    plus more for garnish
2 tablespoons (30 g/1.1 oz)
    unsweetened tomato paste
¼ cup (63 g/2.2 oz) coconut butter or
    almond butter
¼ cup (60 ml) water

To prepare curry paste, place all
the ingredients in a food processor
or a blender. Pulse until smooth.
Set aside.

Rogan Josh Curry Paste:

4 cloves garlic, peeled
1 small (14 g/0.5 oz) red chile pepper,
    halved
2½-inch piece (15 g/0.5 oz) ginger
    root, peeled
1 tablespoon (6 g/0.2 oz) garam
    masala
1 tablespoon (6 g/0.2 oz) paprika
2 teaspoons ground cumin
2 teaspoons ground coriander
1 teaspoon turmeric powder
1 teaspoon smoked paprika
½ teaspoon ground cinnamon
½ teaspoon black pepper
1 teaspoon fine sea salt
1 bunch (30 g/1.1 oz) fresh cilantro,
    plus more for garnish
¼ cup (63 g/2.2 oz) unsweetened
    tomato paste
3 tablespoons (45 ml) water

To prepare curry paste, place all
the ingredients in a food processor
or a blender. Pulse until smooth.
Set aside.

Korma Curry Paste:

4 cloves garlic, peeled

1 small (14 g/0.5 oz) green chile pepper, halved

2½-inch piece (15 g/0.5 oz) ginger root, peeled

2 teaspoons garam masala

2 teaspoons ground cumin

2 teaspoons ground coriander

½ teaspoon turmeric powder

½ teaspoon ground cinnamon

1 teaspoon fine sea salt

¼ to ½ teaspoon cayenne pepper

1 bunch (30 g/1.1 oz) fresh cilantro, plus more for garnish

2 tablespoons (30 g/1.1 oz) unsweetened tomato paste

¼ cup (60 g/2.1 oz) coconut butter or almond butter

2 tablespoons (30 ml) water

To prepare the curry paste, place all the ingredients in a food processor or a blender and pulse until smooth. Place in an airtight container and refrigerate for up to 1 week, or freeze any remaining curry paste in an ice cube tray for up to 3 months. To enhance the flavor, try toasting whole spices. Instead of ground cumin, coriander, and black pepper, you can use whole seeds and toast them in a hot pan for 1 to 2 minutes before blending into a paste with the remaining ingredients. Although curry paste is usually made with oil, you won't use it in most meals because they already contain other high-fat ingredients (ghee, coconut milk, cream, or coconut butter).

CAN'T FIND HEALTHY ALTERNATIVES? MAKE YOUR OWN!

Quick Mayonnaise

Use a wide-mouth mason jar that just about fits the head of your immersion blender. This is vital for the recipe to work. Place 2 large egg yolks, 2 teaspoons Dijon mustard, 2 tablespoons (30 ml) apple cider vinegar, 2 tablespoons (30 ml) fresh lemon juice, ½ teaspoon fine sea salt, and ¼ teaspoon ground black pepper. Pour 1½ cups (360 ml) walnut oil (or macadamia oil or avocado oil) on top, and let it settle for 20 seconds. Place the head of the immersion blender at the bottom of the jar and turn it on high speed. (Do not pulse.) As the mayonnaise starts to thicken, gently tilt and move the head of the immersion blender until the mayonnaise is thick. Add 2 tablespoons (30 ml/1 oz) whey (the liquid part on top of raw full-fat yogurt), or powder from 1 to 2 probiotic capsules. Cover the jar loosely with a lid or a cloth, and let it sit on a kitchen counter for 8 hours. This is essential in order to activate the enzymes that will keep your mayo fresh. Refrigerate after 8 hours, and use within the next 3 months. Try it in Fish & Seafood Bouillabaisse (page 119).

Marinara Sauce

To make a medium jar of marinara sauce (300 g/10.5 oz), you'll need 1 cup (150 g/5.3 oz) cherry tomatoes, ½ cup (20 g/0.7 oz) fresh basil, 2 cloves garlic, 1 small (30 g/1.1 oz) shallot, 4 tablespoons (60 g/2.2 oz) tomato paste, ¼ cup (60 ml) extra-virgin olive oil, ¼ teaspoon salt, and freshly ground pepper to taste. Place all the ingredients in a food processor and blend until smooth. When done, place in an airtight container and store in the fridge for up to 1 week. Try it in One-Pot Cheese-Stuffed Meatballs (page 91).

Sauerkraut

Sauerkraut (a.k.a. pickled, fermented cabbage) is high in vitamin C and very low in carbs. Sauerkraut is beneficial for your digestive system due to its high levels of probiotics and natural digestive enzymes. To make a 1-quart (950-ml) jar of sauerkraut: Cut 1 large head (1 kg/2.2 lb) cabbage into quarters and remove the hard cores. Discard any dry outer leaves. Slice the cabbage with a knife or use a slicing blade on your food processor. Transfer it to a large bowl; sprinkle with 1 tablespoon (17 g/0.6 oz) salt and optionally with 1 tablespoon (7 g/0.3 oz) caraway seeds, about 10 juniper berries, and/or 1 teaspoon mustard seeds. Mix well and let it sit for about 2 hours.

Press and squeeze the cabbage to release as much of the juices as you can. Place the sweated cabbage in a 1-quart (950-ml) Fido jar, leave a small gap, and close it. Don't worry about the jar exploding; the fermentation gases will escape through the rubber lid while no oxygen will get in, thus there will be no risk of failure. Oxygen is what causes mold, so do not open the jar during fermentation. Keep the jar out of direct sunlight and ferment at room temperature, 60° to 75°F (16° to 24°C), for 3 to 5 weeks. When done, refrigerate, and store for up to 6 months or preserve for longer. Try it in Sausage & Cabbage Stew (page 157).

Kimchi

Similar to sauerkraut, kimchi is made through a process called lacto-fermentation and it is good for your gut. To make a 1-quart (950-ml) jar of kimchi: Cut 2 medium (900 g/2 lb) heads of Napa cabbage lengthwise into quarters and remove the cores. Slice each quarter into 1-inch (2.5-cm) strips. Place the sliced cabbage in a large bowl and sprinkle with salt; start with 1 tablespoon (17 g/0.6 oz) and add more if needed. Using your hands, massage the salt into the cabbage to release the juices and soften it. Let the cabbage sit for 20 to 30 minutes.

Once the cabbage has softened, add 6 ounces (170 g) julienned daikon radish, 4 medium (60 g/2.1 oz) sliced spring onions, 4 cloves minced garlic, 2 tablespoons (12 g/0.4 oz) finely chopped fresh ginger, ¼ cup (28 g/1 oz) Korean hot pepper powder, and 1 tablespoon (15 ml) fish sauce. Mix until well combined. (Be sure to wear gloves when handling red pepper flakes.) Optionally, add 2 to 4 tablespoons (20 to 40 g/0.7 to 1.4 oz) of erythritol or Swerve to balance out the spiciness of the chili powder.

Place the vegetables in a sterilized 1-quart (950-ml) Fido jar, pressing down until the brine rises above the vegetables. If there isn't enough juice, add a little salted water until the vegetables are covered. Leave at least 1 inch (2.5 cm) of space between the liquid and the top of the jar, close it, and place on a small tray to catch any juices that may escape during fermentation. Leave the jar in a warm spot in the kitchen to ferment for 3 to 7 days.

The best way to tell whether the kimchi is ready is to taste it during the fermentation process; the longer you leave it, the stronger it'll taste. Once it's done, store in the fridge for up to 6 months. Try it in Korean Beef & Kimchi Stew (page 150).

Cream Cheese

Place 2 cups (480 g) full-fat yogurt into a nut milk bag or cheesecloth, and close the top. Hang on your kitchen counter on a cupboard doorknob over a bowl to collect the whey. You can use the whey to make your mayonnaise stay fresher for longer (page 25). Leave to drain for up to 24 hours. When done, store the cream cheese in an airtight container in the fridge for up to 2 weeks. Try it in Chicken Chowder (page 69).

Pumpkin Purée

Preheat the oven to 300°F (150°C, or gas mark 2). Cut the squash in half and place the halves face down on a baking tray lined with parchment paper. Transfer to the oven and bake for 1 to 1½ hours, until soft. Using a fork, pierce the skin to make sure it's cooked. Remove from the oven and let the squash cool down. Using a spoon, remove the seeds, and scoop the pumpkin meat out into a bowl. Place some of the squash in a piece of cheesecloth and squeeze the excess juices out. (You can reuse them in soups and stews.) Repeat for the remaining squash. Place the squash in a blender and process until smooth. Refrigerate for up to 5 days, or freeze for up to 6 months. Try it in Pumpkin Pie Custard (page 183).

Homemade Nut/Seed Milk

Rinse 1 cup of any nuts or seeds (almonds, cashews, hazelnuts, Brazil nuts, hemp seeds; weight will vary). Transfer them to a bowl. Add 3 cups (720 ml) water and leave to soak for 12 to 24 hours. Strain them through a colander and rinse well with water. Discard the water. Place them in a blender and add 3 cups (720 ml) fresh water. Pulse on high speed until smooth.

Use cheesecloth or a nut milk bag and pour the mixture through it. Squeeze out the milk and discard the pulp, or dehydrate it in the oven and store it in an airtight container. Use just like almond meal. You can leave the milk plain or add any spices or low-carb sweeteners of choice (vanilla, cinnamon, stevia, etc.). Pour the milk into a sealable glass bottle and keep in the fridge for up to 4 days.

Coconut Milk versus "Creamed" Coconut Milk

If a recipe calls for coconut milk, you can either use canned coconut milk (solids + liquids), carton coconut milk, or homemade coconut milk (see below).

If a recipe calls for "creamed" coconut milk, you can either buy ready-made coconut cream or make your own using canned coconut milk. Creamed coconut milk is the fatty part of coconut milk that has separated. To cream coconut milk, simply place the can in the fridge overnight. Open it the next day; do not shake before opening the can. Spoon out the solidified coconut milk and discard the liquids. One 13.5 ounce (400 ml) can will yield about 7 ounces (200 grams) of coconut cream.

Homemade Coconut Milk

Place 3 cups (230 g/8 oz) shredded desiccated coconut in a blender, and add 4 to 5 cups (940 ml to 1.2 L) boiling water. Blend on high for 45 to 60 seconds. When done, pour the mixture through a cheesecloth or nut milk bag. Squeeze out the milk and reserve the pulp for future uses. Once the pulp is dry, you can blend it to make fine coconut flour or use it just like desiccated coconut. When the milk is done, add any spices or sweeteners of choice. Pour into a sealable glass bottle. Store in the fridge for up to 2 days and shake well before use.

Homemade Nut, Seed, and Coconut Butter

Place 4 cups (weight will vary) of whole nuts, seeds, or shredded coconut or 5 cups (400 g) flaked coconut in a strong food processor. Process for several minutes, until smooth. Depending on the butter, this will take anywhere between 1 and 8 minutes. High-fat macadamia butter will take about 2 minutes, while coconut butter will take up to 8 minutes. Using a spatula, scrape the butter from the sides several times, as needed. Store at room temperature for up to 1 month.

Homemade Stocks

Stocks are available in most grocery stores, but there is nothing quite like a warming cup of freshly made stock or broth. Both stock and bone broth can be used interchangeably, although they are technically not the same thing. Bone broth (page 44) requires up to ten times longer cooking time and contains higher levels of gelatin. If you're short on time, stock is a great alternative to bone broth. Each of the following recipes will yield 9 to 10 cups (about 2 L) of stock.

Vegetable Stock

2 tablespoons (30 g/1.1 oz) ghee or virgin coconut oil
3 medium (180 g/6.4 oz) carrots, peeled and roughly chopped
4 large (256 g/9 oz) celery stalks, roughly chopped
1 small (150 g/3.5 oz) celeriac, peeled and roughly chopped
1 large (150 g/3.5 oz) yellow onion, halved, skin on
8 cloves garlic, peeled and halved
1 bunch fresh parsley
5 to 6 sprigs thyme
3 bay leaves
1 to 2 teaspoons fine sea salt
Handful of dried porcini mushrooms
2.6 quarts (2.5 L) water

Grease a large saucepan with the ghee. Roast the vegetables and seasonings over medium-high heat for 5 to 10 minutes, stirring frequently. Optionally, add the dried mushrooms, pour in the water, and transfer to a slow cooker. Cook on high for 2 hours or on low for 4 hours. Strain the stock through a muslin-lined sieve into another saucepan and let it cool. Store in the fridge for up to 5 days, or freeze for up to 6 months.

Chicken Stock

3 to 4 pounds (1.4 to 1.8 kg) chicken bones and cartilages (use leftovers from roasts)
1 large (150 g/3.5 oz) yellow onion, halved, skin on
2 medium (120 g/4.2 oz) carrots, peeled and cut into thirds
2 large (128 g/4.5 oz) celery stalks
4 cloves garlic, peeled and halved
3 bay leaves
1 teaspoon whole black peppercorns
2.6 quarts (2.5 L) water

Place all the ingredients in a slow cooker. Cook on high for 4 hours or on low for 8 hours. Strain the stock through a muslin-lined sieve into another saucepan and let it cool. Store in the fridge for up to 4 days, or freeze for up to 3 months.

Seafood/Fish Stock

1½ pounds (680 g) seafood shells (shrimp, lobster, crab), or 3 to 4 pounds (1.4 to 1.8 kg) fish bones
   and heads
1 large (150 g/3.5 oz) yellow onion, halved, skin on
3 large (192 g/6.8 oz) celery stalks
4 cloves garlic, peeled and halved
2 tablespoons (30 g/1.1 oz) unsweetened tomato paste
2 teaspoons fine sea salt
1 teaspoon whole black peppercorns
2 bay leaves
5 to 6 sprigs fresh thyme
2.6 quarts (2.5 L) water

To enhance the flavor, you can optionally roast the seafood shells in the oven preheated to 400°F (200°C, or gas mark 6) for 10 to 12 minutes. Place all the ingredients in a slow cooker. Cook on high for 2 hours or on low for 4 hours. Strain the stock through a muslin-lined sieve into another saucepan and let it cool. Store in the fridge for up to 3 days, or freeze for up to 3 months.

For more homemade condiments and keto staples such as ketchup, mustard, and Sriracha sauce, visit ketodietapp.com/blog.

QUICK KETO HACKS

Eat Lean Meat Cuts with Healthy Fats

Lean meat cuts are naturally high in protein, but it doesn't mean you have to avoid them. If you cook with lean meat cuts such as chicken, white fish, and seafood, simply serve them with healthy fats such as mayonnaise (page 25), Aioli (page 119), Spicy Hollandaise (page 137), avocado, butter, or cheese.

Thickening Sauces and Gravies

If you are preparing a dish on the stove, you can thicken sauces by reducing them (cooking the sauce until part of the water evaporates). To avoid overcooking other ingredients, such as meat and vegetables, use tongs to transfer them to a plate and return them when the sauce has thickened to a desired consistency. You can even reduce the sauce directly in the slow cooker by removing the lid and cooking on high for 30 to 45 minutes.

- Egg yolks work amazingly well if you need to thicken soups and stews without adding extra carbs. I use about 1 egg yolk per every cup (240 ml) of liquids (water, stock, or cream), or less if a recipe includes other ingredients, such as tomato paste, heavy whipping cream, or coconut milk. To make this simple thickener, mix the required number of egg yolks in ½ to 1 cup (120 to 240 ml) cold liquids and slowly drizzle into the pot at the end of the cooking process while stirring. Try in Hungarian Goulash (page 74).

- Ground chia seeds work well for thickening sauces. To avoid any unwanted "jelly" texture, use just 1 to 2 tablespoons (8 to 16 g/0.3 to 0.6 oz) of ground chia seeds and sprinkle them into the dish while stirring at the end of the cooking process.

- Coconut butter (or any nut and seed butter) works amazingly well in curries. Adding just 2 to 4 tablespoons (30 to 60 g/1.1 to 2.1 oz) makes them creamy and delicious. You can add them at the beginning of the cooking process. If you're adapting a recipe for your slow cooker for the first time and you are not quite sure about how much to use, add it gradually at the end of the cooking process.

- Coconut flour, almond flour, and other nut and seed flours work well for thickening sauces. Depending on the recipe, use 2 to 4 tablespoons (weight will vary) and stir in at the end of the cooking process.

- Heavy whipping cream, sour cream, cream cheese, and hard cheese make your sauces and soups creamy. Beware that some dairy products will separate if cooked for a prolonged period of time. You should add them in the last 15 to 30 minutes of the cooking process, or after the cooking has finished. Try in Broccoli Cheese Soup (page 57).

- Coconut milk and coconut cream are great dairy-free options in recipes that call for regular cream. Just like dairy, add coconut milk and cream at the end of the cooking process.

- Blending or part-blending veggies will thicken soups and gravies. Simply ladle half of the vegetables into a bowl and set aside. Use an immersion blender to purée the remaining vegetables in the pot, and then place the reserved vegetables back into the pot. Try in Ratatouille Soup (page 59). My Creamy "Potato" Soup (page 63) uses dried mushrooms that help with thickening when blended.

- Glucomannan powder, also known as konjak powder, is made from the same ingredient as shirataki (a.k.a. "zero-carb" noodles). Depending on the desired thickness, you will need about ½ to 1 teaspoon of glucomannan powder for every cup (240 ml) of liquids. Simply mix it in a small amount of water and slowly drizzle into the pot while stirring.

PRECOOKED KETO STAPLES

Poached Eggs

Fill a medium saucepan with water and a dash of vinegar. Bring to a boil over high heat. Crack each egg individually into a ramekin or a cup. Using a spoon, create a gentle whirlpool in the water. Slowly lower the egg into the water in the center of the whirlpool. Turn off the heat and cook for 3 to 4 minutes. Use a slotted spoon to remove the egg from the water and place it on a plate. Repeat for all remaining eggs and set aside.

Serve immediately or refrigerate in an airtight container for up to 5 days. To reheat the eggs, place them in a mug filled with hot tap water for a couple of minutes. This will be enough to warm them up without overcooking. Try them in Mushroom & Dill Sour Soup (page 60).

Crispy Bacon

Place the bacon slices in a large pan and add ½ cup (120 ml) water. Cook over medium-high heat until the water starts to boil. Reduce the heat to medium and cook until the water evaporates and the bacon fat is rendered. Reduce the heat to low, and cook until the bacon is lightly browned and crispy. Crumble and use the crisped-up bacon for topping. Reserve the cooking fat for another recipe; it can be used just like ghee or lard. Try it in Chicken Chowder (page 69).

KETO COOKING & ALCOHOL

If you follow the ketogenic diet to lose weight, then you know that alcohol should be avoided completely. Although pure alcohol doesn't contain carbs, drinking alcohol will slow weight loss. Even if there is no sugar, your body cannot simply store alcohol as fat—it has to metabolize it. This means that it will use alcohol instead of body fat. Additionally, it will slow your progress if your aim is to build muscle mass.

So should alcohol be avoided in cooking? Not necessarily. You can use dry red or white wine for cooking because most of the alcohol will evaporate. It does not cook out the alcohol completely, but the remaining content after several hours of slow cooking is negligible. The longer you cook your meal for, the less alcohol your meal will retain. In most slow-cooked meals, you will remove 95 percent of the original alcohol content, leaving the amazing flavor intact.

If you want to avoid alcohol completely, you can try the following substitutions:
1 cup (240 ml) dry red wine = ¾ cup + 2 tablespoons (210 ml) bone broth (page 44) plus 2 tablespoons (30 ml) red wine vinegar, apple cider vinegar, or lemon juice

1 cup (240 ml) dry white wine = ¾ cup + 2 tablespoons (210 ml) chicken stock (page 28) plus 2 tablespoons (30 ml) white wine vinegar, apple cider vinegar, or lemon juice

USE NATURAL LOW-CARB SWEETENERS

Sugar is sugar. No matter how healthy the sweetener is, it will always impair your weight loss and kick you out of ketosis. When you follow a ketogenic diet, you need to eliminate high-carb sweeteners such as table sugar, high-fructose corn syrup, honey, maple syrup, and coconut palm sugar. All these will raise your blood sugar and kick you out of ketosis, even when you use small amounts. Sweeteners to avoid also include the seemingly healthy agave syrup. Agave is 90 percent fructose and has damaging effects on our metabolism.

Beware that not all low-carb sweeteners are healthy. Artificial sweeteners, such as aspartame and sucralose, should be avoided. Certain sugar alcohols, including maltitol and sorbitol, should also be avoided. Furthermore, stay away from foods and sweeteners containing dextrose and maltodextrin, as they are known to raise blood sugar. (Beware that some stevia and monk fruit sweetener blends use dextrose and maltodextrin to bulk up!)

I always use only natural low-carb sweeteners: stevia, erythritol, Swerve, monk fruit, and a small amount of yacon syrup. Although some low-carbers use xylitol, it is known to cause stomach discomfort and I personally avoid it because I can't tolerate it.

Stevia

Stevia is an herb and is commonly known as "sugar leaf." The extract from this herb is used as a sweetener and sugar substitute because it has zero effect on blood sugar and contains no calories. Liquid stevia and stevia powder are 200 to 300 times sweeter than sugar; use very small amounts to avoid a bitter aftertaste. The general rule is to use no more than 3 to 5 drops per serving. There are other types of stevia products, including stevia glycerite (about twice as sweet as sugar with gooey texture), and granulated stevia-and-erythritol blends.

Erythritol and Swerve

Erythritol is naturally found in fruits, vegetables, and fermented foods. It is a sugar alcohol that does not affect blood glucose and has zero calories. Ninety percent of erythritol is absorbed before it enters the large intestine and is excreted via urine. Unlike xylitol, it doesn't cause stomach discomfort when used within the recommended amounts. Swerve is a brand sweetener that is made with a blend of erythritol and prebiotic fibers called fructooligosaccharides. While Swerve is as sweet as sugar and can be used in a 1:1 ratio, erythritol has about 70 percent of the sweetness of table sugar.

Monk Fruit

Monk fruit, also known as luo han guo or longevity fruit, is a fruit native to China and northern Thailand. It's 300 times sweeter than sugar and has been used in traditional Chinese medicine to treat obesity and diabetes. It's as sweet as stevia, but without the bitter aftertaste. It's available in both liquid and powdered form. Just like stevia, it's found in some brand sweeteners where it's combined with erythritol. Avoid products that additionally contain dextrose or maltodextrin.

Yacon Syrup

Yacon syrup is extracted from the yacon plant grown in South America. The root has been used for its nutritional and medicinal purposes for hundreds of years. It's made via natural evaporation, and it has a slight caramel taste that is similar to blackstrap molasses. Although it's low in carbs, it's not a zero-carb sweetener and you should be using small amounts, such as 1 to 2 tablespoons (15 to 30 ml) per recipe.

Using Low-Carb Sweeteners

The amount of sweeteners you use depends on your palate. You may need to add or reduce the amount of sweeteners used in recipes. I personally don't use the equivalent of sugar in most recipes, and I use a lot less because I would find them too sweet. If you are an experienced low-carber, then you will likely feel the same way. As you get used to low-carb eating, you will use smaller amounts of sweeteners, or even avoid them altogether. On the other hand, if you just started following a low-carb diet, then you may find some recipes not sweet enough. You can add a few extra drops of stevia or a little more erythritol to suit your palate.

Keep in Mind the Following Conversions:

1 cup (200 g/7.1 oz) of granulated stevia or monk fruit blend = 1 teaspoon of powdered or liquid stevia or liquid monk fruit

1 tablespoon (10 g/0.4 oz) of sugar = 6 to 9 drops of liquid or ¼ teaspoon of powdered stevia or monk fruit

1 teaspoon of sugar = 2 to 4 drops of liquid or a pinch of powdered stevia or monk fruit

1 cup (200 g/7.1 oz) granulated Swerve = 1 cup table sugar

1 cup (120 g/4.2 oz) powdered Swerve = 1 cup (120 g/4.2 oz) powdered sugar

1⅓ cups (267 g/9.4 oz) erythritol = 1 cup (267 g/9.4 oz) table sugar

2 tablespoons (40 g/1.4 oz) yacon syrup = 1 tablespoon (20 g/0.7 oz) blackstrap molasses or honey

ALLERGY-FRIENDLY SWAPS

1 cup (240 ml) heavy whipping cream = 1 cup (240 ml) coconut milk

1 cup (240 g/8.5 oz) mascarpone cheese = 1 cup (240 g/8.5 oz) creamed coconut milk (coconut cream) (see page 27)

1 cup (100 g/3.5 oz) almond flour = ⅓ cup (40 g/1.4 oz) coconut flour, plus increase liquids (eggs, nut milk, cream, etc.)

1 large egg = 1 tablespoon (7 g/0.2 oz) ground flaxseed or 1 tablespoon (8 g/0.3 oz) ground chia seeds or 1 tablespoon (7 g/0.2 oz) gelatin powder, mixed with 3 tablespoons (45 ml) of water (limited use, as it won't work for mayonnaise, Hollandaise, or Sourdough Keto Buns, page 52)

1 cup (250 g/8.8 oz) almond butter = 1 cup (250 g/8.8 oz) coconut butter or any seed butter
1 tablespoon (15 g/0.5 oz) ghee or butter = 1 tablespoon (15 g/0.5 oz) lard, tallow, duck fat, goose fat, or virgin coconut oil

STORING FOOD IN THE FREEZER

Cooked chicken, beef, pork, and lamb can be stored in the fridge for up to 4 days. Store cooked seafood in the fridge for up to 3 days. They all can be frozen for up to 3 months. If you're planning to use frozen meat and fish in your slow cooker, let it slowly defrost in the fridge. Do not leave raw meat on the kitchen counter.

The following foods you should never freeze and should always prepare fresh and keep refrigerated:

- Raw vegetables: cabbage (do not freeze your Coleslaw, page 141), celery, cucumbers, radishes, bean sprouts, peppers, and leafy greens (such as arugula, lettuce, and watercress)

- Soft herbs such as basil, chives, parsley, and cilantro

- Dairy and other similar foods with high water content: cream cheese, cream, coconut milk, and coconut cream

- Other foods such as cooked egg whites and mayonnaise (page 25)

How to Use This Book

When you're sourcing ingredients, try to get them in their most natural forms. That is, organically grown and free from unnecessary additives. Buy organic eggs, organic unwaxed lemons, pastured beef and butter, outdoor-reared pork, wild-caught fish, and extra-virgin coconut oil.

Remember:

- Nutrition values for each recipe are per serving unless stated otherwise. The nutrition data are derived from the USDA National Nutrient Database (ndb.nal.usda.gov).

- Nutrition facts are calculated from edible parts. For example, if one medium green pepper is listed as 120 g/4.2 oz, this value represents its edible parts (seeds and stalk removed) unless otherwise specified.

- Optional ingredients and suggested sides and toppings are not included in the nutrition information.

- All slow cooker recipes have been prepared in a large 6-quart (5.7-L) slow cooker. While most recipes will work in a smaller or larger slow cooker, some recipes will require you to use a large 5- to 6-quart (4.7- to 5.7-L) slow cooker to fit all the ingredients. These recipes always mention that you will need a 5- to 6-quart (4.7- to 5.7-L) slow cooker.

- Recipes that are allergy-free are marked with the appropriate tags:

dairy-free   nut-free   Additionally, when a recipe includes an

egg-free   vegetarian   allergy-free option, it is tagged with ⟨⟩, ⟨⟩, and accordingly.

AN IMPORTANT NOTE ABOUT MEASUREMENTS

If you are following a ketogenic diet for specific health reasons, you should be aware that accuracy is vital in order for this diet to work. When measuring ingredients, always weigh them using a kitchen scale. Using measures like cups or tablespoons can lead to inaccuracies that may affect the macronutrient composition of your meal. All it takes to shift your body out of ketosis is a few extra grams of carbohydrates. Plus, cups and tablespoons for dried products (flax meal, etc.) may vary depending on the brand.

Chapter 2

HOMEMADE BASICS & STAPLES

If you could see my fridge and freezer, you would always find condiments and basic ingredients I use regularly. And there is a good reason for it—I make most of them myself. They are easy to prepare and budget-friendly, and I never have to worry about added sugar, gluten, and other unwanted ingredients. Still not convinced? Even if you can find "clean" products, chances are they will cost three times more than homemade.

This chapter features my favorite keto staples that I use in recipes throughout this book, from easy-to-make keto condiments, such as pesto, BBQ sauce, and curry paste, to low-carb sides, including creamy cauli-mash, rustic sourdough bread, and even tortillas. These recipes go hand in hand with the stews, roasts, and casseroles!

Red Pesto

I use homemade pesto almost every day, so I always keep a jar on hand in the fridge. It takes just a few minutes to prepare, and adds zing to everything from casseroles to soups to salads.

Ingredients

- ¼ cup (25 g/0.9 oz) pitted green or black olives
- ½ cup (67 g/2.4 oz) macadamia nuts
- 2 tablespoons (20 g/0.7 oz) pine nuts
- 1 cup (110 g/3.9 oz) sun-dried tomatoes, drained
- 6 cloves garlic, peeled and sliced
- 1 tablespoon (15 ml) fresh lemon juice or apple cider vinegar
- ¼ cup (63 g/2.2 oz) unsweetened tomato paste
- 2 cups (30 g/1.1 oz) fresh basil leaves
- ½ cup (120 ml) extra-virgin olive oil
- ¼ teaspoon fine sea salt
- ¼ teaspoon black pepper
- Optional: ½ cup (45 g/1.6 oz) grated Parmesan cheese

Instructions

Place all the ingredients in a food processor and pulse until smooth. Alternatively, use a mortar and pestle to crush all the ingredients into a smooth paste. Transfer to a jar and refrigerate. You can keep your pesto in the fridge for up to 1 week or two if it's stored properly. It helps to pour a thin layer of olive oil on the top, as it keeps it fresh longer. Whenever you use the pesto, remember to add another thin layer of olive oil before you put it back in the fridge.

TIP: If you want to make this pesto nut-free, instead of macadamia nuts and pine nuts, use an equal amount of sunflower seeds. It's better if you use soaked and dehydrated nuts or seeds.

To preserve pesto for longer, spoon it into an ice cube tray and place in the freezer. Once frozen, empty the ice cube tray into a resealable plastic bag. Keep your frozen pesto cubes for up to 6 months.

NUTRITION FACTS PER TABLESPOON (15 G/0.5 OZ):
Total carbs: 1.6 g / Fiber: 0.5 g / Net carbs: 1.1 g / Protein: 0.5 g / Fat: 6.1 g / Energy: 61 kcal
Macronutrient ratio: Calories from carbs (7%), protein (4%), fat (89%)

Harissa Paste

Made from red peppers, chiles, and spices, this North African paste is so versatile. I use it as a meat marinade, with cauli-rice, and mixed with full-fat yogurt as a keto-friendly salad dressing. Use a combination of your favorite chiles, and adjust the amount of harissa you use in your recipes according to its heat.

Ingredients

HARISSA PASTE:

2 medium (240 g/8.5 oz) red peppers
5 ounces (140 g) dried chiles of choice (any combination of guajillo, New Mexico, ancho, chipotle, arbol)
4 to 6 pieces (28 g/1 oz) sun-dried tomatoes, drained
6 cloves garlic, peeled
1 teaspoon ground turmeric
2 teaspoons fine sea salt
¼ cup (60 ml) extra-virgin olive oil
Juice from 1 lemon (about 60 ml/¼ cup)

SPICES FOR TOASTING:

1 teaspoon whole coriander seeds
1 teaspoon whole cumin seeds
1 teaspoon whole caraway seeds

Instructions

Roast the bell peppers in an oven preheated to 350°F (175°C, or gas mark 4). Bake for 30 to 40 minutes, or until the skin is charred and the peppers are soft. Remove from the oven. Put a piece of baking foil over the peppers and set aside to cool until they are easy to handle. Peel the skin and remove the seeds.

While the peppers are baking, place the dried chiles in a pot and cover with 2 cups (480 ml) boiling water. Cover with a lid and let them sit for 20 to 30 minutes. Drain the chiles, and discard the stems and seeds.

Place the coriander, cumin, and caraway seeds in a hot pan and dry-roast briefly for just a minute or two. Grind the spices in a mortar and pestle or a coffee grinder.

Place all ingredients in a food processor or blender: chiles, bell peppers, toasted spices, sun-dried tomatoes, garlic, turmeric, salt, olive oil, and lemon juice. Process until smooth, spoon into a jar, and store in the fridge for up to 1 week. To preserve harissa for longer, spoon it into an ice cube tray and place in the freezer. Once frozen, empty the ice cube tray into a resealable plastic bag. Keep your frozen harissa cubes for up to 6 months.

TIP: Use a combination of your favorite chiles. A combination of fresh, sweet, bell peppers with guajillo, ancho, and chipotle chiles results in moderate-mild spicy harissa. If you prefer more heat, add some arbol chiles or skip the bell peppers. Don't forget to adjust the amount of harissa used in recipes to adjust for the heat.

NUTRITION FACTS PER TABLESPOON (15 G/0.5 OZ):
Total carbs: 2.9 g / Fiber: 1.1 g / Net carbs: 1.8 g / Protein: 0.3 g / Fat: 2 g / Energy: 29 kcal
Macronutrient ratio: Calories from carbs (27%), protein (9%), fat (64%)

Thai Curry Paste

Toss a few ingredients in the blender, and you'll have a freezer-friendly Thai curry sauce that lasts for months. A single tablespoon makes sauces creamier and boosts flavor without adding a ton of carbs!

Ingredients

3 medium (150 g/5.3 oz) shallots or brown onion

2 heads (50 g/1.8 oz) garlic, about 16 cloves

⅓ cup (80 g/2.8 oz) sliced ginger root

2 tablespoons (12 g/0.4 oz) fresh sliced turmeric or 2 teaspoons turmeric powder

Juice and zest from 1 lime (about 3 tablespoons/45 ml)

2 lemongrass stalks

10 to 20 pieces (40 g/1.4 oz) green or red Thai chiles

1 tablespoon (5 g/0.2 oz) coriander seeds

1 teaspoon whole peppercorns, white or mixed

2 teaspoons cumin seeds

2 tablespoons (30 ml) fish sauce or coconut aminos

1 teaspoon ground cinnamon

1 teaspoon fine sea salt

¼ cup (10 g/0.4 oz) fresh cilantro, or to taste

Instructions

Peel and roughly chop the shallots, garlic, ginger, and turmeric root. Zest and juice the lime. Remove the outer woody lemongrass stalk; only use the soft bulb inside. Cut the stems off the chiles and remove the seeds (or keep some if you prefer your curry paste extra hot).

Place the coriander seeds, peppercorns, and cumin seeds in a hot pan and dry-roast briefly for just 30 to 60 seconds. Place all the ingredients in a food processor or blender and process until smooth. Spoon the paste into a jar and store in the fridge for up to 1 week. Freeze any remaining curry paste in an ice cube tray and store for up to 3 months.

NUTRITION FACTS PER TABLESPOON (15 G/0.5 OZ):
Total carbs: 2.6 g / Fiber: 0.5 g / Net carbs: 2.1 g / Protein: 0.4 g / Fat: 0.1 g / Energy: 12 kcal
Macronutrient ratio: Calories from carbs (76%), protein (16%), fat (8%)

Sweet & Sour BBQ Sauce

This sweet, tangy, easy-to-prepare BBQ sauce is the perfect way to dress up juicy ribs, fork-tender pulled pork, and comforting meat stews.

Ingredients

- 2 tablespoons (30 g/1.1 oz) ghee or other healthy cooking fat (see page 14)
- 1 large (150 g/5.3 oz) yellow onion, peeled and diced
- 4 cloves garlic, peeled and minced
- 2 pieces (28 g/1 oz) jalapeño peppers, seeds and core removed
- 1½ cups (360 g/12.7 oz) canned tomatoes
- ½ cup (125 g/4.4 oz) unsweetened tomato paste
- ½ cup (120 ml) apple cider vinegar or coconut vinegar
- ¼ cup (60 ml) coconut aminos
- ¼ cup (50 g/1.8 oz) granulated erythritol or Swerve
- 2 teaspoons paprika, sweet or smoked
- 2 teaspoons mustard powder
- 1 teaspoon celery seeds
- ½ teaspoon chili powder
- ½ teaspoon black pepper
- ⅛ teaspoon ground cloves
- ⅛ teaspoon ground allspice
- 1 teaspoon fine sea salt, or to taste
- 2 teaspoons extra-virgin olive oil
- Optional: few drops of liquid stevia

Instructions

Preheat your slow cooker to low. In a pan greased with ghee, cook the onion over medium-low heat for about 10 minutes, until browned and fragrant. Add the garlic and cook for another minute.

Place the browned onion and garlic in the preheated slow cooker. Add all the remaining ingredients, apart from the olive oil, and cook for 6 hours. When done, turn off the heat and let it cool for an hour. Add the olive oil. Using a blender, process the sauce until smooth. Transfer to a glass jar and keep in the fridge for up to a month. For longer storage, spoon the sauce into an ice cube tray and freeze for 2 hours. Place in a bag and store in the freezer for up to 6 months.

NUTRITION FACTS PER TABLESPOON (15 G/0.5 OZ):
Total carbs: 1 g / Fiber: 0.2 g / Net carbs: 0.8 g / Fat: 1 g / Energy: 13 kcal
Macronutrient ratio: Calories from carbs (23%), protein (5%), fat (72%)

Cranberry Sauce

This spiced, sugar-free cranberry sauce is an all-rounder: it works well in both sweet and savory recipes. Try serving it alongside roast turkey at the holidays; mix it into full-fat yogurt as a snack; or use it as a cheesecake topping.

Ingredients

1.3 pounds (600 g) cranberries, fresh or frozen

Juice and zest from 1 medium (150 g/5.3 oz) orange

1 cup (240 ml) water

⅔ cup (133 g/4.7 oz) granulated erythritol or Swerve

20 to 30 drops liquid stevia

1 teaspoon ground cinnamon or 2 to 3 cinnamon sticks

½ teaspoon vanilla powder or 2 teaspoons unsweetened vanilla extract

½ teaspoon ginger powder

¼ teaspoon ground cloves

Instructions

Preheat your slow cooker to high. Place all the ingredients in the slow cooker, cover with a lid, and cook for 3½ hours. Remove the lid and mix. Cook uncovered for another 30 minutes. When done, mix, let it cool, and place it in jars. Store in the fridge for up to 2 weeks. For longer storage, spoon into an ice cube tray and freeze for 2 to 3 hours. Place in a bag and freeze for up to 6 months.

TIPS: A small amount of orange juice will have no significant effect on carbs per serving. If you prefer to avoid it, you can use ¼ cup (60 ml) lemon or lime juice instead.

For a richer flavor, you can substitute ½ cup (120 ml) water with ½ cup (120 ml) of dry red wine (see page 31 for information about alcohol).

If you don't like your sauce chunky, spoon it into a blender and pulse until smooth.

NUTRITION FACTS PER TABLESPOON (20 G/0.7 OZ):
Total carbs: 2.1 g / Fiber: 0.6 g / Net carbs: 1.5 g / Protein: 0.1 g / Fat: 0 g / Energy: 8 kcal
Macronutrient ratio: Calories from carbs (92%), protein (5%), fat (3%)

MAKES: 6 to 8 cups
PREPARATION TIME: 10 minutes
COOKING TIME: 2 hours or more

Bone Broth

Homemade bone broth is both tasty and high in healthy gelatin and minerals. (And it's great for keeping keto-flu at bay, too!) Give your Bone Broth an antioxidant and anti-inflammatory boost by adding a little turmeric to the mix.

Ingredients

- 2 medium (120 g/4.2 oz) carrots, peeled and cut into thirds
- 1 large (150 g/5.3 oz) white onion, halved
- 4 to 6 cloves garlic, halved
- 2 large (128 g/4.5 oz) celery stalks, cut into thirds
- 3.3 pounds (1.5 kg) oxtail or assorted bones (chicken feet, marrowbones, etc.)
- 2 tablespoons (30 ml/1 fl oz) apple cider vinegar or lemon juice
- 3 bay leaves
- 3 whole allspice
- 1 tablespoon (17 g/0.6 oz) fine sea salt
- 2-inch (5 cm) piece turmeric, sliced, or 1 teaspoon turmeric powder
- 8 to 10 cups (1.9 to 2.4 L/64 to 81 fl oz) water (enough to cover the bones, no more than ⅔ the capacity of the pressure cooker, ¾ of the Dutch oven, or ¾ of the slow cooker)

Instructions

Place all the ingredients in the slow cooker. Cover with a lid. Cook on high for 4 to 5 hours or on low for 8 to 10 hours. Remove the oxtail using tongs and shred the meat using a fork (use the cooked meat for quick meals). Place the bones back in the slow cooker and cook on low for up to 48 hours (optional but highly recommended). Once the broth has cooled, strain it through a sieve, and store it without any bones, spices, or vegetables. Keep it in the fridge if you're planning to use it over the next 4 to 5 days. For future uses, store it in small containers and freeze.

TIP: Oxtail is high in fat, and the greasy layer on top—the tallow—will solidify. Simply scrape most of the tallow off and discard or reuse it for cooking.

NUTRITION FACTS PER CUP (240 ML):
Total carbs: 0.9 g / Fiber: 0.2 g / Net carbs: 0.7 g / Protein: 3.6 g / Fat: 6 g / Energy: 72 kcal
Macronutrient ratio: Calories from carbs (4%), protein (20%), fat (76%)
Note: Nutrition facts, especially protein, in homemade bone broth vary and depend on several factors, such as type of bones used and cooking time.

Make-Ahead Freezer Meatballs

I love the convenience of these simple, all-purpose meatballs. They take just a few minutes to make, and they can go straight from the freezer into a hearty stove-top sauce for a no-fuss, low-carb meal.

Ingredients

4.4 pounds (2 kg) ground beef

1 medium (110 g/3.9 oz) onion, finely chopped

4 cloves garlic, crushed

¼ cup (15 g/0.5 oz) freshly chopped herbs of choice (parsley, basil, oregano, cilantro, etc.), or 1 tablespoon dried herbs

1½ teaspoons fine sea salt

½ teaspoon black pepper

Optional: 1 cup (90 g/3.2 oz) grated Parmesan cheese

Instructions

Place all the ingredients in a bowl and combine well. Using your hands, create 64 medium-sized meatballs (about 34 g/1.2 oz each).

Place the meatballs on a tray or baking sheet in a single layer and freeze for 1½ to 2 hours. Place the meatballs in a bag and store in the freezer for up to 3 months. When ready to be used in a recipe, place the required amount of meatballs in the fridge to defrost overnight. Alternatively, add frozen meatballs directly to sauces and cook on the stove (see Quick Meatball Casserole, page 144).

TIP: Make your own meatballs or patties (flattened meatballs) using any ground meat (beef, pork, lamb, chicken, turkey, etc.), and mix it with your favorite herbs and spices such as parsley, basil, oregano, cilantro, paprika, cumin, coriander, or chile flakes. You can even add 1 to 2 tablespoons (15 to 30 g) of Red Pesto (page 37)!

NUTRITION FACTS PER SERVING (4 MEATBALLS):
Total carbs: 0.9 g / Fiber: 0.2 g / Net carbs: 0.7 g / Protein: 21.6 g / Fat: 25 g / Energy: 322 kcal
Macronutrient ratio: Calories from carbs (1%), protein (27%), fat (72%)

MAKES: 10 tortillas
PREPARATION TIME: 20 minutes
COOKING TIME: 20 minutes + chilling

Keto Tortillas Three Ways

These tortillas are based on one of the most popular recipes on my blog, and with good reason: they're just like the real thing! Soft and flexible, they're ideal with pulled pork, roasted vegetables, and avocado slices.

Ingredients

BASIC INGREDIENTS:

1 cup (100 g/3.5 oz) almond flour

¾ cup (113 g/4 oz) flax meal

¼ cup (30 g/1.1 oz) coconut flour

2 tablespoons (8 g/0.3 oz) whole psyllium husks

2 tablespoons (15 g/0.5 oz) ground chia seeds

1 teaspoon fine sea salt

2 tablespoons (30 g/1.1 oz) ghee or other healthy cooking fat (see page 14)

FOR SPINACH TORTILLAS:

2 cups (312 g/11 oz) frozen spinach, thawed, drained, and puréed

1 teaspoon ground cumin

¾ cup (180 ml) lukewarm water, plus a few tablespoons if the dough is too dry

FOR PESTO TORTILLAS:

3 tablespoons (45 g/1.6 oz) Red Pesto (page 37)

½ cup (45 g/1.6 oz) grated Parmesan

1 cup (240 ml) lukewarm water, plus a few tablespoons if the dough is too dry

Instructions

Combine all the basic ingredients, apart from the cooking fat. Add all the other ingredients needed to make spinach, pesto, or curried tortillas. (If making spinach tortillas, drain the frozen spinach and discard the excess water. Place in a blender and process until puréed.) If the dough is too dry to roll, add a few more tablespoons of water. Mix well using your hands and shape into an oval. Let the dough rest in the fridge for up to 1 hour.

When ready, remove the dough from the fridge and cut it into 6 equal pieces. (You will make the remaining 4 tortillas using the excess dough.) Place a piece of the dough between 2 pieces of parchment paper and roll it out until very thin. Alternatively, use a silicone roller and a silicone mat.

Remove the top parchment paper. Press a large 8-inch (20-cm) lid into the dough (or use a piece of parchment paper to cut into a round shape). Trace around it with your knife to cut out the tortilla.

Repeat for the remaining pieces of dough. Add the cut-off excess dough to the last piece and create the remaining 4 tortillas from it. If you have any dough left over, simply roll it out and cut it into tortilla-chip shapes.

Grease a large pan with ghee and cook 1 tortilla at a time for 2 to 3 minutes on each side over medium heat until lightly browned. Don't overcook it: it'll become too crispy. Once cool, store the tortillas in an airtight container for up to 1 week and reheat them in a dry pan, if needed.

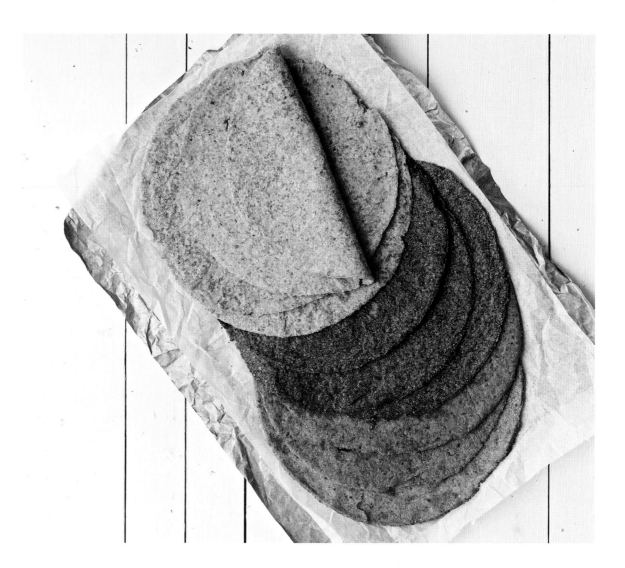

FOR CURRIED TORTILLAS:

2 tablespoons (30 g/1.1 oz) curry paste (pages 23–24)

1 cup (240 ml) lukewarm water, plus a few tablespoons if the dough is too dry

Tip: It works with Harissa Paste (page 39) too!

TIP: To make taco shells, cut small pieces of parchment paper and place the tortillas on top. Fold over a rack in the oven and turn the oven on. Make sure you make them wide enough so you can fit the filling in later. Cook until the oven reaches 400°F (200°C, or gas mark 6) and then cook for 5 to 8 minutes, or until crispy.

NUTRITION FACTS PER TORTILLA (SPINACH/PESTO/CURRIED):
Total carbs: 8.7/7.9/7.8 g / Fiber: 6.7/5.9/5.8 g / Net carbs: 2/2/2 g / Protein: 6.2/6.8/5.1 g
Fat: 14.2/17/14 g / Energy: 176/202/168 kcal
Macronutrient ratio: Calories from carbs (5/4/5%), protein (15/15/13%), fat (80/81/82%)

Make-Ahead Slow Cooker Mash

Laden with fresh herbs, slow-cooker cauliflower mash is the perfect side for your stews and casseroles. It freezes well, too, so go ahead and make a big batch. For a super-creamy version, add 1 cup (240 g/8.5 oz) cream cheese or sour cream just before blending.

Ingredients

- 2 to 3 heads (2 kg/4.4 lb) cauliflower, cut into florets
- 8 cups (1.9 L) water, or enough to cover the cauliflower
- 2 teaspoons fine sea salt, plus more to taste
- 1 teaspoon whole peppercorns
- 2 bay leaves
- 3 whole allspice
- ½ cup (110 g/3.9 oz) ghee or other healthy cooking fat (see page 14)
- 1 large (150 g/5.3 oz) yellow onion, sliced
- 4 cloves garlic, minced
- ¼ cup (15 g/0.5 oz) freshly chopped herbs of choice (parsley, dill, thyme, rosemary, etc.)

Instructions

Preheat a 5- to 6-quart (4.7- to 5.7-L) slow cooker. Place the cauliflower florets, water, salt, peppercorns, bay leaves, and allspice in the slow cooker (use a spice bag to easily remove the spices). Cover with a lid. Cook on high for 3 to 4 hours or on low for 6 to 8 hours.

Grease a skillet with the ghee. Add the onion and cook over medium-high heat for about 10 minutes, or until golden brown. Add the garlic and cook for another minute. When done, take off the heat and set aside.

When the cauliflower is tender, turn the slow cooker off and drain the water by pouring it through a colander. Discard the spices. Place the cauliflower back in the slow cooker and process with an immersion blender for a chunky texture. Or purée in batches in a food processor for a creamy texture. Add the cooked onion and garlic, including the ghee, and process to combine. Taste and season with more salt and pepper if needed. Add the fresh herbs and stir in until combined.
Eat as a side with meat, or let it cool down and store in an airtight container for up to 5 days. To store for longer, spoon into single- or double-serving freezer bags.

NUTRITION FACTS PER SERVING (ABOUT ¾ CUP/180 G/6.4 OZ):
Total carbs: 9.8 g / Fiber: 3.7 g / Net carbs: 6.1 g / Protein: 3.4 g / Fat: 9.7 g / Energy: 131 kcal
Macronutrient ratio: Calories from carbs (20%), protein (11%), fat (69%)

TIPS: Bored of plain cauli-mash? Skip the bay leaves and allspice and try the following variations:

- Super creamy mash: add 1 cup (240 g/8.5 oz) cream cheese or sour cream just before blending.

- Italian pesto mash: add ½ cup (120 g/4.2 oz) Red Pesto (page 37).

- Lemon & herb mash: add 2 to 3 teaspoons (4 to 6 g) fresh lemon zest and a bunch of fresh basil leaves.

- Curried mash: add 1 tablespoon (6 g/0.2 oz) curry powder and a small bunch of cilantro.

Cauliflower Rice Three Ways

Skip the starchy sides and make keto-friendly (and vitamin-C-rich) cauliflower rice instead: it's the perfect partner for slow-cooked meat and flavorful sauces. Just add your favorite spices and you're good to go!

Ingredients

1 medium (720 g/1.6 lb) cauliflower

2 tablespoons (30 g/1.1 oz) ghee or other healthy cooking fat (see page 14)

Salt and freshly ground black pepper

MASALA CAULI-RICE:

1 teaspoon garam masala

½ teaspoon onion powder

¼ teaspoon turmeric powder

⅛ teaspoon chili powder

LEMON & HERB CAULI-RICE:

2 tablespoons (8 g/0.3 oz) fresh herbs such as basil, oregano, thyme, and parsley

1 teaspoon fresh lemon zest

½ teaspoon garlic powder

SPANISH CAULI-RICE:

½ teaspoon onion powder

½ teaspoon garlic powder

2 tablespoons (30 g/1.1 oz) tomato paste

Instructions

Run the cauliflower florets through a hand grater or food processor with a grating blade. Pulse until the florets resemble grains of rice. (See instructions on page 18.)

Grease a large saucepan with ghee and add all the aromatics for the preferred cauli-rice recipe: Masala, Lemon & Herb, or Spanish. Mix and cook over medium-low heat for up to 1 minute. Add the cauliflower rice and cook for 5 to 7 minutes, stirring constantly. Season with salt and pepper, and serve with slow-cooked meat and sauce. To store, let it cool and place in an airtight container. Refrigerate for up to 5 days.

NUTRITION FACTS PER SERVING (ABOUT 1 CUP MASALA/LEMON & HERB/SPANISH CAULI-RICE):
Total carbs: 9.6/9.4/10.2 g / Fiber: 3.8/3.7/3.9 g / Net carbs: 5.8/5.7/6.3 g / Protein: 3.6/3.6/3.7 g
Fat: 8.1/8/8 g / Energy: 116/115/118 kcal
Macronutrient ratio: Calories from carbs (21/21/23%), protein (13/13/13%), fat (66/66/64%)

MAKES: 8 regular or 16 mini buns
PREPARATION TIME: 15 minutes
COOKING TIME: 40 to 45 minutes

Sourdough Keto Buns

This is the absolute best bread recipe I've ever come across—low-carb or otherwise! These buns are fluffy and flavorful, and taste just like the loaves of rustic bread my grandma used to make.

Ingredients

DRY INGREDIENTS:

1½ cups (150 g/5.3 oz) almond flour
⅓ cup (40 g/1.4 oz) psyllium husk powder
½ cup (60 g/2.1 oz) coconut flour
½ cup (75 g/2.6 oz) flax meal
1 teaspoon baking soda
1 teaspoon fine sea salt

WET INGREDIENTS:

6 large egg whites (Reserve egg yolks for Mushroom & Dill Sour Soup, page 60.)
2 large eggs
¾ cup (180 g/6.5 oz) low-fat buttermilk (see tips)
¼ cup (60 ml) apple cider vinegar
1 cup (240 ml) lukewarm water

Instructions

Preheat the oven to 350°F (180°C, or gas mark 4). Mix all the dry ingredients in a bowl. In a separate bowl, mix the egg whites, eggs, and buttermilk. Add the egg mixture to the dry mixture, and process well using a mixer until the dough is thick. Add the vinegar and lukewarm water, and process until well combined. Do not overprocess the dough. Using a spoon, make 8 regular or 16 mini buns. Place them on a baking tray lined with parchment paper or a nonstick mat, leaving some space between them.

Transfer them to the oven and bake for 10 minutes. Reduce the temperature to 300°F (150°C, or gas mark 2) and bake for another 30 to 45 minutes (small buns will take less time to cook). Remove from the oven, let them cool, and place the buns on a rack to cool to room temperature. Store them at room temperature if you plan to use them in the next couple of days or store in the freezer for up to 3 months.

NUTRITION FACTS PER MINI BUN:
Total carbs: 7 g / Fiber: 4.8 g / Net carbs: 2.2 g / Protein: 6.1 g / Fat: 8.2 g / Energy: 116 kcal
Macronutrient ratio: Calories from carbs (8%), protein (23%), fat (69%)

TIPS:

- For best results, use a kitchen scale to weigh all the dry ingredients.

- Do not use full-fat buttermilk or the buns will end up too dense.

- I've always had best results when using whole psyllium husks that I powder myself in a coffee grinder. Store-bought psyllium husk powder will work, too, but the buns may be denser. Baked goods that use psyllium always result in a slightly moist texture. If needed, cut the buns in half and place in a toaster or in the oven before serving.

- To save time, mix all the dry ingredients ahead and store in a resealable bag and add a label with the number of servings. When ready to be baked, just add the wet ingredients!

- Looking for dairy-free, nut-free, flax-free, or psyllium-free options? Check out my blog at ketodietapp.com/blog and search for "bread."

Chapter 3

SATISFYING & NOURISHING SOUPS

There is nothing more comforting than a hot bowl of hearty soup on a chilly, rainy day. And soups are not just for winter! Recipes included in this chapter can be enjoyed throughout the year: comforting chowders and hearty pumpkin soup to chase away the fall's chill; or tangy coconut laksa and refreshing ratatouille soup that highlight summer's bounty of fresh vegetables. They are easy, simple, and perfect for feeding hungry crowds. They are also nutritious enough to be enjoyed as complete meals. While many can be made on the stove in less than 30 minutes, some are best prepared low and slow in a slow cooker.

Chicken Mulligatawny Soup

MAKES: 6 servings
PREPARATION TIME: 10 minutes
COOKING TIME: 35 minutes

Never heard of mulligatawny soup? You're in for a treat. This classic Anglo-Indian curried soup turns up on Indian restaurant menus all over the UK, and it's full of warming, invigorating spices, like cumin, coriander, and turmeric.

Ingredients

2 tablespoons (30 g/1.1 oz) coconut oil or other healthy cooking fat (see page 14)

1 small (70 g/2.5 oz) yellow onion, diced

1 medium (85 g/3 oz) leek or 4 to 6 baby leeks, sliced

3 large (192 g/6.8 oz) celery stalks, sliced

1 tablespoon (5 g/0.2 oz) ground cumin

1 tablespoon (5 g/0.2 oz) ground coriander

1 teaspoon turmeric powder

1 teaspoon garam masala

2 cups (480 ml) coconut milk

3 cups (720 ml) chicken stock (page 28)

1 pound (450 g) boneless chicken thighs, sliced

2½ cups (300 g/10.6 oz) uncooked cauli-rice (page 18)

Salt and pepper

Fresh cilantro for garnish

Optional: ⅓ cup (30 g/1.1 oz) toasted flaked almonds

Instructions

In a large heavy-based pot greased with coconut oil, cook the onion over medium-high heat for 5 to 8 minutes, until lightly browned. Add the leek and celery, and cook for 2 minutes. Add the cumin, coriander, turmeric, garam masala, coconut milk, stock, and chicken thighs. Bring to a boil, cover with a lid, and simmer for about 20 minutes. Add the cauli-rice and cook uncovered over medium heat for 5 minutes. Season with salt and pepper to taste.

To serve, garnish with fresh cilantro, and optionally top with flaked almonds. To store, let it cool, and refrigerate in an airtight container for up to 4 days or freeze for up to 3 months.

TIP: Swap chicken with raw shrimp and add them in the last 2 to 3 minutes of the cooking process.

NUTRITION FACTS PER SERVING (1½ CUPS/360 ML):
Total carbs: 9.6 g / Fiber: 2.6 g / Net carbs: 7 g / Protein: 20.2 g / Fat: 27.2 g / Energy: 352 kcal
Macronutrient ratio: Calories from carbs (8%), protein (23%), fat (69%)

Broccoli Cheese Soup

Cheesy, creamy, and filling, this simple, starch-free soup is even better than the traditional version. And you won't miss the flour one bit: blending fresh vegetables with Cheddar cheese ensures a deliciously thick and silky result.

Ingredients

- 1 medium (300 g/10.6 oz) broccoli
- ½ medium (300 g/10.6 oz) cauliflower
- 2 tablespoons (30 g/1.1 oz) ghee or other healthy cooking fat (see page 14)
- 1 medium (110 g/3.9 oz) yellow onion, chopped
- 2 cloves garlic, minced
- 1 medium (85 g/3 oz) leek, sliced
- 2 large (128 g/4.5 oz) celery stalks, sliced
- 4 cups (1.2 L) vegetable stock or chicken stock (page 28)
- 3 cups (720 ml) water
- 1 cup (240 ml) heavy whipping cream
- 2 cups (226 g/8 oz) shredded Cheddar cheese
- 2 tablespoons (8 g/0.3 oz) freshly chopped parsley, plus more for garnish
- Salt and pepper

Instructions

Preheat a 5- to 6-quart (4.7- to 5.7-L) slow cooker. Cut the broccoli and cauliflower into florets. Peel and roughly chop the broccoli stalks. Heat a skillet greased with ghee over medium-high heat. Add the onion and cook for 5 to 8 minutes, until lightly browned, stirring frequently. Add the garlic, leek, and celery. Cook for 1 to 2 minutes.

Place in the slow cooker, and add the cauliflower and broccoli pieces, vegetable stock, and water. Cover with a lid. Cook on high for 2 to 3 hours or on low for 4 to 6 hours.

Slowly pour in the cream while stirring. Add the Cheddar cheese and parsley (keep some cheese and parsley for garnish). Use an immersion blender and process until puréed, smooth or chunky. If using a regular blender, let the soup cool for 15 to 20 minutes (hot liquids can be dangerous!). Season with salt and pepper to taste, and garnish with the reserved cheese and parsley. To store, let it cool, and refrigerate in an airtight container for up to 5 days or freeze for up to 3 months.

NUTRITION FACTS PER SERVING (ABOUT 1½ CUPS/360 ML):
Total carbs: 8.6 g / Fiber: 2.3 g / Net carbs: 6.3 g / Protein: 10.3 g / Fat: 30.2 g / Energy: 344 kcal
Macronutrient ratio: Calories from carbs (7%), protein (12%), fat (81%)

Ratatouille Soup

Some soups, like this delicate version of ratatouille, are best prepared on the stovetop, with ingredients added gradually. It features pesto and fresh herbs, which contain volatile oils: to preserve their flavors, they should be added at the end of the cooking process.

Ingredients

SOUP:

2 tablespoons (30 g/1.1 oz) ghee or other healthy cooking fat (see page 14)

1 small (110 g/3.9 oz) yellow onion, chopped

2 cloves garlic, minced

1 medium (120 g/4.2 oz) green pepper, diced

1 medium (120 g/4.2 oz) yellow or orange pepper, diced

1 medium (200 g/7.1 oz) zucchini, diced (you can use leftover zucchini cores from "Apple" Pie Crumble, page 180)

1 medium (250 g/8.8 oz) eggplant, diced

1 teaspoon dried oregano

14.1 ounces (400 g) canned diced tomatoes

2 cups (480 ml) vegetable stock or chicken stock (page 28)

2 cups (480 ml) water

2 tablespoons (30 g/1.1 oz) Red Pesto (page 37)

Salt and pepper

TOPPING:

6 oz (170 g) fresh mozzarella di bufalla

6 tablespoons (90 ml) extra-virgin olive oil to serve

Fresh basil for garnish

Instructions

Heat a skillet greased with ghee over medium heat. Add the onion and cook over medium-high heat for 5 to 8 minutes, until lightly browned. Add the garlic, peppers, zucchini, and eggplant. Cook for 1 to 2 minutes, stirring frequently. Add the oregano, tomatoes, vegetable stock, and water. Bring to a boil and cook over medium heat for about 15 minutes, or until the vegetables are tender. Take off the heat.

Use a ladle to transfer half of the vegetables to a bowl and set aside. Use an immersion blender to purée the remaining vegetables. Place the reserved vegetables back into the pot and add the pesto. Stir and season with salt and pepper.

To serve, ladle the soup into serving bowls and top with a piece of fresh mozzarella cheese. Drizzle each bowl with a tablespoon (15 ml) of olive oil and garnish with basil leaves. To store, let it cool, and refrigerate in an airtight container for up to 5 days or freeze for up to 3 months (without the topping).

NUTRITION FACTS PER SERVING (ABOUT 1½ CUPS/360 ML):
Total carbs: 11.9 g / Fiber: 3.7 g / Net carbs: 8.2 g / Fat: 29.1 g / Energy: 338 kcal
Macronutrient ratio: Calories from carbs (10%), protein (11%), fat (79%)

MAKES: 6 servings
PREPARATION TIME: 15 minutes
COOKING TIME: 25 minutes

Mushroom & Dill Sour Soup

This recipe is based on a traditional Czech soup called kulajda: beloved by home cooks, it turns up on restaurant menus all over the Czech Republic once the weather starts to turn chilly. Heavy cream and egg yolks make it extremely filling, but they're balanced out by palate-lifting dill, caraway, and vinegar.

Ingredients

SOUP:

5 cups (1.2 L) chicken stock or vegetable stock (page 28)

1 medium (400 g/14.1 oz) rutabaga, peeled and cut into 1-inch (2.5-cm) pieces

2 bay leaves

3 whole allspice

4 cups (216 g/7.6 oz) wild mushrooms, such as chanterelle, sliced

½ teaspoon caraway seeds

½ teaspoon fine sea salt, or to taste

½ cup (120 ml) heavy whipping cream

6 egg yolks

1 cup (230 g/8.1 oz) full-fat sour cream

¼ cup (15 g/0.5 oz) freshly chopped dill, plus more for garnish

2 to 4 tablespoons (30 to 60 ml) white wine vinegar

TOPPING:

6 large poached eggs

Black pepper or chili powder

Instructions

Heat the stock in a large heavy-based pot over medium-high heat. Once boiling, reduce the heat to medium and add the rutabaga, bay leaves, and allspice. Cover with a lid and cook for about 15 minutes. Add the wild mushrooms, caraway seeds, and salt. Cook, covered, for another 5 minutes, or until the rutabaga is tender. Remove the lid and reduce the heat to low.

In a bowl, whisk the heavy whipping cream and egg yolks. Slowly pour the mixture into the pot, stirring constantly, until the soup thickens. Take off the heat and discard the bay leaves. Slowly stir in the sour cream, and add the dill and vinegar to taste. Season with salt and pepper.

To serve, ladle the soup into serving bowls and top with poached eggs (see page 30). Garnish with dill, pepper, or chili powder. To store, let it cool, and store in an airtight container in the fridge for up to 5 days. Serve with gently reheated poached eggs. To store for longer, freeze for up to 3 months (without the topping).

NUTRITION FACTS PER SERVING (ABOUT 1½ CUPS/360 ML):
Total carbs: 11.4 g / Fiber: 3.1 g / Net carbs: 8.3 g / Protein: 15.5 g / Fat: 28.8 g / Energy: 368 kcal
Macronutrient ratio: Calories from carbs (9%), protein (18%), fat (73%)

Creamy "Potato" Soup

The Czech Republic is a country of soups. Czechs eat soups on just about every occasion and at any time of the day—as a starter or main dish, and even for breakfast. This is a low-carb version of yet another family recipe: rutabaga makes a great substitute for starchy potatoes here.

Ingredients

½ cup (15 g/0.5 oz) dried porcini
   mushrooms
⅓ cup (73 g/2.6 oz) ghee or
   other healthy cooking fat (see
   page 14)
1 small (70 g/2.5 oz) yellow onion
2 large (128 g/4.5 oz) celery
   stalks, sliced
1 small (60 g/2.1 oz) carrot,
   peeled and sliced
2 cloves garlic, minced
1 small (500 g/1.1 lb) cauliflower,
   chopped into florets
1 medium (400 g/14.1 oz)
   rutabaga, peeled and cut into
   1-inch (2.5-cm) pieces
1 teaspoon fine sea salt, or to
   taste
¼ teaspoon black pepper
7 cups (1.7 L) water
2 bay leaves
2 teaspoons dried marjoram
1 teaspoon caraway seeds
2 tablespoons (8 g/0.3 oz) freshly
   chopped parsley

Instructions

Place the mushrooms in a cup filled with a cup (240 ml) of water and soak for 30 minutes. In a large heavy-based pot or casserole dish greased with ghee, cook the onion over medium-high heat for 5 to 8 minutes, until lightly browned. Add the celery, carrot, and garlic, and cook for another minute. Add the cauliflower, rutabaga, soaked mushrooms including their water, salt, pepper, water, bay leaves, marjoram, and caraway seeds. Bring to a boil, and then reduce the heat to medium-low and cook, covered, for about 20 minutes.

Take off the heat and let it cool for 10 to 15 minutes. Discard the bay leaves, ladle half of the vegetables into a bowl, and set aside. Use an immersion blender and process the remaining vegetables and stock until smooth. Add back the reserved vegetables and parsley. Season to taste and eat immediately, or let it cool and refrigerate in an airtight container for up to 5 days or freeze for up to 3 months.

NUTRITION FACTS PER SERVING (ABOUT 1½ CUPS/360 ML):
Total carbs: 11.3 g / Fiber: 3.4 g / Net carbs: 7.9 g / Protein: 2.3 g / Fat: 9.6 g / Energy: 135 kcal
Macronutrient ratio: Calories from carbs (25%), protein (7%), fat (68%)

MAKES: 6 servings
PREPARATION TIME: 15 minutes
COOKING TIME: 25 minutes

Salmon Chowder

This fragrant salmon chowder is very low in carbs—no potatoes or flour necessary!—and high in heart-healthy omega-3 fats. And it's a guaranteed crowd-pleaser on snowy, wintery nights.

Ingredients

- 1½ pounds (680 g) skinless salmon or canned salmon
- 2 tablespoons (30 g/1.1 oz) ghee or other healthy cooking fat (see page 14)
- 1 medium (110 g/3.9 oz) yellow onion, diced
- 3 cloves garlic, minced
- 1 medium (120 g/4.2 oz) yellow bell pepper, sliced
- 2 large (128 g/4.5 oz) celery stalks, sliced
- 1 medium (200 g/7.1 oz) zucchini, diced
- 3 cups (720 ml) fish stock (page 29), clam juice, or chicken stock (page 28)
- 2 bay leaves
- 1½ cups (360 ml) heavy whipping cream or coconut milk
- 2 tablespoons (30 ml) fresh lemon juice
- 2 tablespoons (8 g/0.3 oz) freshly chopped dill
- ¾ teaspoon fine sea salt, or to taste
- Ground black pepper

Instructions

Dice the salmon into about 1-inch (2.5-cm) pieces (or add the canned salmon at the end of the cooking process). In a large heavy-based pot greased with ghee, cook the onion over medium-high heat for 5 to 8 minutes, stirring frequently. Add the garlic, pepper, celery, and zucchini. Add the stock and bay leaves, bring to a boil, and cook, covered, over medium-low heat for about 8 minutes, or until the vegetables are tender. Reduce the heat to low, add the salmon, and slowly pour in the cream. Once simmering, cook for 5 to 7 minutes, or until the salmon is cooked through and begins to break up.

Remove the bay leaves, and add the lemon juice, dill, salt, and pepper to taste. To store, let it cool, and place in an airtight container in the fridge for up to 4 days or freeze for up to 3 months.

NUTRITION FACTS PER SERVING (1½ CUPS/360 ML)):
Total carbs: 26.9 g / Fiber: 1.6 g / Net carbs: 5.3 g / Protein: 29.1 g / Fat: 37.2 g / Energy: 487 kcal
Macronutrient ratio: Calories from carbs (5%), protein (25%), fat (70%)

Smoked Haddock & Squash Chowder

Full of colorful, low-carb vegetables and protein-rich fish, this inventive take on fish chowder is a cheerful, one-bowl meal. If you can't find smoked haddock fillets, use regular ones instead, and sprinkle with ¼ teaspoon of smoked fine sea salt before using.

Ingredients

- 4 medium (60 g/2.1 oz) spring onions, white and green parts separated
- 2 tablespoons (30 g/1.1 oz) ghee or other healthy cooking fat (see page 14)
- 3 cloves garlic, minced
- 3 cups (720 ml) fish stock (page 29), clam juice, or chicken stock (page 28)
- 2 bay leaves
- 1½ pounds (680 g) skinless smoked haddock or cod fillets (undyed)
- 1 medium (85 g/3 oz) leek, sliced
- 2 large (128 g/4.5 oz) celery stalks, sliced
- 1 cup (100 g/3.5 oz) green beans, cut into thirds
- 2 cups (232 g/8.2 oz) pumpkin cut into 1-inch (2.5-cm) pieces
- 1½ cups (360 ml) heavy whipping cream or coconut milk
- 2 tablespoons (8 g/0.3 oz) freshly chopped dill or parsley, plus more for garnish
- Salt and pepper

Instructions

Slice the spring onions and reserve the green tips for garnish. In a large heavy-based saucepan greased with ghee, cook the white part of the onion over medium heat for 2 to 3 minutes, stirring frequently. Add the garlic and cook for a minute. Add the stock and bay leaves, and bring to a boil. Add the haddock fillets, reduce the heat to low, and cook for 5 minutes. Use a slotted spoon to remove the fillets onto a plate and set aside. Once cool, flake the fish into smaller pieces.

To the saucepan, add the leek, celery stalks, green beans, and pumpkin. Cook over medium heat for 10 minutes, until the green beans are tender. Slowly pour in the cream, cook for 1 to 2 minutes, and then turn off the heat. Discard the bay leaves.

Ladle half of the cooked vegetables into a bowl and set aside. Using an immersion blender, purée the remaining vegetables and stock. Add back the reserved vegetables and flaked haddock. Mix in the fresh dill, and season with salt and pepper to taste. To serve, garnish with the remaining green parts of the spring onions and dill. To store, let it cool, and refrigerate in an airtight container for up to 4 days or freeze for up to 3 months.

NUTRITION FACTS PER SERVING (1½ CUPS/360 ML):
Total carbs: 9.3 g / Fiber: 1.6 g / Net carbs: 7.7 g / Protein: 33.5 g / Fat: 31.5 g / Energy: 461 kcal
Macronutrient ratio: Calories from carbs (7%), protein (30%), fat (63%)

Chicken Coconut Laksa

Laksa is a tangy, spicy soup popular in Malaysia and Singapore, and this keto-friendly version gets a special kick from homemade Thai Curry Paste (page 40). As with my Chicken Mulligatawny Soup (page 55), you can use raw shrimp in place of the chicken, if you like: just add them in the last 2 to 3 minutes of cooking.

Ingredients

- 2 tablespoons (30 g/1.1 oz) virgin coconut oil or other healthy cooking fat (see page 14)
- 1 small (70 g/2.5 oz) yellow onion, diced
- 2 cloves garlic, minced
- 1.3 pounds (600 g) skinless chicken thighs, sliced
- ½ cup (120 g/4.2 oz) Thai Curry Paste (page 40)
- 3 cups (720 ml) chicken stock or vegetable stock (page 28)
- 2 cups (480 ml) coconut milk
- 2 cups (100 g/3.5 oz) wild Asian mushrooms such as shiitake, sliced
- 2 tablespoons (30 ml) fish sauce
- 2 tablespoons (30 ml) fresh lime juice
- 2 medium (400 g/14.1 oz) zucchini or daikon radish, spiralized (see page 18)
- Salt and pepper
- Fresh cilantro for garnish

Instructions

In a large heavy-based saucepan greased with coconut oil, cook the onion over medium-high heat for 5 to 8 minutes, until lightly browned. Add the garlic and cook for a minute. Add the chicken and curry paste, and cook for about 3 minutes while stirring. Pour in the stock and coconut milk, and bring to a boil. Lower the heat and simmer, covered, for another 10 minutes.

Add the mushrooms and cook for 5 minutes. Add the fish sauce, lime juice, and zucchini noodles. Cook for 2 to 4 more minutes. Take off the heat, season to taste with the salt and pepper, and serve with fresh cilantro for garnish. To store, let it cool, and refrigerate in an airtight container for up to 4 days or freeze for up to 3 months (without the zucchini noodles).

TIP: Swap chicken with raw shrimp and add them in the last 2 to 3 minutes of the cooking process.

NUTRITION FACTS PER SERVING (ABOUT 1½ CUPS/360 ML):
Total carbs: 10.6 g / Fiber: 1.9 g / Net carbs: 8.7 g / Protein: 25.4 g / Fat: 28 g / Energy: 383 kcal
Macronutrient ratio: Calories from carbs (9%), protein (26%), fat (65%)

Chicken Chowder

This family-friendly chicken chowder is incredibly creamy and sating, since it's full of protein and healthy fats. And since you can do most of the prep the night before, it makes an ideal weeknight dinner.

Ingredients

2 tablespoons (30 g/1.1 oz) duck fat or other healthy cooking fat (see page 14)

1 medium (110 g/3.9 oz) yellow onion, sliced

1.3 pounds (600 g) skinless chicken thighs, cubed

1 teaspoon fine sea salt, or to taste

½ teaspoon white or black pepper

1 medium (80 g/2.8 oz) carrot, peeled and sliced

2 large (128 g/4.5 oz) celery stalks, sliced

3 cloves garlic, minced

2 cups (200 g/7.1 oz) green beans, trimmed and cut into thirds

2 medium (400 g/14.1 oz) turnips, peeled and cut into 1-inch (2.5-cm) pieces

2 bay leaves

1 teaspoon dried thyme

1 teaspoon oregano

1 cup (240 g/8.5 oz) full-fat cream cheese

3 cups (720 ml) chicken stock (page 28) or bone broth (page 44)

2 cups (480 ml) water

1½ cups (360 ml) heavy whipping cream

6 large (180 g/6.3 oz) slices bacon, crisped up and crumbled (see page 31)

Fresh parsley or chives for garnish

Instructions

Preheat the slow cooker. In a large heavy-based saucepan greased with ghee, cook the onion over medium-high heat for 5 to 8 minutes, until lightly browned. Add the chicken and cook until browned on all sides, 1 to 2 minutes, stirring frequently. Season with salt and pepper, and transfer to the slow cooker.

Add the carrot, celery, garlic, green beans, turnips, bay leaves, thyme, oregano, cream cheese, chicken stock, and water. Cook on high for 3 to 4 hours or on low for 6 to 8 hours. Add the cream in the last 30 minutes of the cooking process. Discard the bay leaves. To serve, pour into serving bowls, and top with bacon and garnish with fresh herbs. To store, let it cool, and refrigerate in an airtight container for up to 4 days or freeze for up to 3 months.

NUTRITION FACTS PER SERVING (ABOUT 1½ CUPS/360 ML):
Total carbs: 10.5 g / Fiber: 2.7 g / Net carbs: 7.8 g / Protein: 23.6 g / Fat: 40 g / Energy: 485 kcal
Macronutrient ratio: Calories from carbs (6%), protein (19%), fat (75%)

Pumpkin & Chorizo Meatball Soup

Pumpkin—a great source of beta-carotene and vitamin A—shines in autumnal treats like pies and cakes, but it's wonderful in savory dishes, too. Smoky chorizo really sets off pumpkin's sweetness in this earthy, low-carb, Mexican-inflected soup.

Ingredients

- 2 tablespoons (30 g/1.1 oz) duck fat or other healthy cooking fat (see page 14)
- 1 small (70 g/2.5 oz) yellow onion, sliced
- 2 cloves garlic, minced
- 4 cups (350 g/12.3 oz) diced pumpkin
- ½ medium (300 g/10.6 oz) cauliflower, cut into florets
- 2 cups (480 ml) chicken stock (page 28) or bone broth (page 44)
- 3 cups (720 ml) water
- 2 teaspoons oregano, preferably Mexican
- 1 teaspoon ground cumin
- 1.1 pounds (500 g) Mexican chorizo
- ½ teaspoon fine sea salt, or to taste
- Ground black pepper
- Fresh cilantro or oregano for garnish
- 3 tablespoons (45 ml) extra-virgin olive oil

Instructions

In a large heavy-based pot greased with ghee, cook the onion over medium-high heat for 5 to 8 minutes, until lightly browned. Add the garlic and cook for a minute. Add the pumpkin, cauliflower florets, stock, water, oregano, and cumin. Bring to a boil and cook, covered, over medium-low heat until the vegetables are tender, 10 to 12 minutes.

Make 12 medium-size meatballs from the chorizo (about 42 g/1.5 oz each), and set aside. After 10 to 12 minutes, take the soup off the heat and let it cool for 5 to 10 minutes. Use an immersion blender and pulse until smooth and creamy. Be careful not to get burned! Return to the burner, add the meatballs to the pot, and bring to a boil. Simmer for 12 to 15 minutes. Season with salt and pepper to taste.

To serve, pour into bowls (3 meatballs per serving), garnish with fresh herbs, and drizzle with olive oil (about ½ tablespoon/ 7 ml per serving). To store, let it cool, and place in an airtight container in the fridge for up to 5 days. To store for longer, let it cool and pour into freezer bags. Freeze for up to 3 months.

NUTRITION FACTS PER SERVING (ABOUT 1¼ CUPS/300 ML, PLUS 3 MEATBALLS):
Total carbs: 10.7 g / Fiber: 2.9 g / Net carbs: 7.8 g / Protein: 16.8 g / Fat: 30.1 g / Energy: 375 kcal
Macronutrient ratio: Calories from carbs (8%), protein (18%), fat (74%)

Hamburger Soup

Craving a juicy burger? Don't head to the nearest fast-food joint: make a batch of this meaty—and highly kid-friendly—soup instead! It's got all the flavors you love in a classic burger, minus the unhealthy carbs.

Ingredients

3 tablespoons (45 g/1.6 oz) ghee or other healthy cooking fat (see page 14)

1 medium (110 g/3.9 oz) yellow onion, chopped

3 cloves garlic, minced

1½ pounds (680 g) ground beef

½ teaspoon fine sea salt, or to taste

¼ teaspoon black pepper

⅛ teaspoon cayenne pepper

½ teaspoon dried thyme

½ teaspoon oregano

3 cups (720 ml) bone broth (page 44) or chicken stock (page 28)

3 cups (720 ml) water

1 cup (240 g/8.5 oz) canned chopped tomatoes

3 tablespoons (45 g/1.6 oz) unsweetened tomato paste

1 teaspoon Dijon mustard

1 medium (400 g/14.1 oz) rutabaga, peeled and cut into 1-inch (2.5-cm) pieces

1 large (64 g/2.3 oz) celery stalk, sliced

1 medium (120 g/4.2 oz) green bell pepper, diced

1 small (74 g/2.6 oz) red bell pepper, diced

1 small (74 g/2.6 oz) yellow bell pepper, diced

1 cup (143 g/5 oz) diced pickled cucumbers

2 tablespoons (8 g/0.3 oz) chopped parsley

Instructions

In a large heavy-based pot greased with ghee, cook the onion over medium-high heat for 5 to 8 minutes, until lightly browned. Add the garlic and cook for a minute. Crumble in the beef and season with the salt, black pepper, and cayenne pepper. Add the thyme and oregano, and mix until lightly browned on all sides. Add the broth, water, tomatoes, tomato paste, Dijon mustard, and rutabaga.

Bring to a boil, cover with a lid, reduce the heat, and simmer for about 15 minutes. Add the celery, peppers, and pickled cucumbers. Cook, uncovered, for another 5 minutes, or until the vegetables are tender. Taste and season with salt if needed. Garnish with the parsley before serving. To store, let it cool, and refrigerate in an airtight container for up to 4 days or freeze for up to 3 months.

Do You Have Thyroid Issues? Make Sure You Cook Your Veggies!

Certain foods such as rutabaga, turnip, broccoli, cauliflower, kohlrabi, Brussels sprouts, and cabbage, are known as goitrogens. If eaten on a regular basis, goitrogens may disrupt the production of thyroid hormones by interfering with iodine uptake in the thyroid gland. Luckily, these veggies are only goitrogenic in the raw state. Cooking, light steaming, or even fermenting deactivates and diminishes their goitrogenic activity.

NUTRITION FACTS PER SERVING (ABOUT 1½ CUPS/360 ML):
Total carbs: 10.5 g / Fiber: 3 g / Net carbs: 7.5 g / Protein: 17.6 g / Fat: 24.1 g / Energy: 328 kcal
Macronutrient ratio: Calories from carbs (10%), protein (22%), fat (68%)

Hungarian Goulash

Creamy, comforting goulash has its roots in Eastern Europe, but it's gained world-wide popularity—not least because it's simple to prepare, easy on the budget, and a hassle-free way to make a hungry crowd very, very happy.

Ingredients

3 tablespoons (45 g/1.6 oz) ghee or other healthy cooking fat (see page 14)

1 large (150 g/5.3 oz) yellow onion, chopped

2 cloves garlic, minced

2 pounds (900 g) beef chuck steak, cut into 1½ inch (4-cm) chunks

1 teaspoon fine sea salt, or to taste

½ teaspoon black pepper

½ teaspoon caraway seeds

½ cup (55 g/1.9 oz) paprika, divided

¼ cup (63 g/2.2 oz) unsweetened tomato paste

2 bay leaves

10 cups (2.4 L) water, divided

1 medium (300 g/10.6 oz) rutabaga, peeled and cut into 1-inch (2.5-cm) pieces

2 medium (240 g/8.5 oz) green bell peppers, sliced

6 egg yolks

2 tablespoons (8 g/0.3 oz) freshly chopped parsley, plus more for garnish

Optional: Sourdough Keto Buns (page 52)

Instructions

In a large heavy-based saucepan or a Dutch oven greased with ghee, cook the onion over medium-high heat for 5 to 8 minutes, until lightly browned. Add the garlic and beef, and cook over medium-high heat, until browned on all sides. Reduce the heat to medium and add the salt, pepper, caraway seeds, and 2 tablespoons (14 g) of the paprika. Add the tomato paste, bay leaves, and 9 cups (2.1 L) of the water. Reduce the heat to low, cover with a lid, and cook for about 90 minutes.

After 90 minutes, add the rutabaga and cook, covered, for another 20 minutes. Add the peppers, and cook for 5 minutes, or until the rutabaga is tender. Add the remaining 6 table-spoons (41 g) paprika to the pot.

Whisk the remaining 1 cup (240 ml) water with the egg yolks. Slowly drizzle in the egg and water, and cook while stirring until it thickens. Take off the heat and let it sit for 5 minutes before serving, garnished with parsley. Goulash pairs perfectly with Sourdough Keto Buns! To store, let it cool, and refrigerate in an airtight container for up to 4 days or freeze for up to 3 months.

NUTRITION FACTS PER SERVING (ABOUT 1½ CUPS/360 ML):
Total carbs: 11.5 g / Fiber: 4.4 g / Net carbs: 7.1 g / Protein: 25.7 g / Fat: 30.3 g / Energy: 418 kcal
Macronutrient ratio: Calories from carbs (7%), protein (25%), fat (68%)

Mexican Chili Soup

MAKES: 6 servings
PREPARATION TIME: 15 minutes
COOKING TIME: 25 minutes

If you're a heat-seeking spice fiend like me, you'll love this low-carb take on chili, featuring the perfect blend of nourishing beef, sweet tomatoes, fiery chiles, and warming spices.

Ingredients

- 2 tablespoons (30 g/1.1 oz) duck fat or other healthy cooking fat (see page 14)
- 1 small (70 g/2.5 oz) yellow onion, chopped
- 2 cloves garlic, minced
- 1 piece (14 g/0.5 oz) jalapeño pepper, sliced
- 1.1 pounds (500 g) ground beef
- ¾ teaspoon fine sea salt, or to taste
- ¼ teaspoon black pepper
- 2 teaspoons ground cumin
- 1 teaspoon chipotle powder
- 1 teaspoon smoked paprika
- 2 tablespoons (30 g/1.1 oz) unsweetened tomato paste
- 1 cup (240 g/8.5 oz) canned chopped tomatoes
- 4 cups (960 ml) bone broth (page 44) or chicken stock (page 28)
- 2 cups (480 ml) water
- 2 medium (240 g/8.5 oz) green bell peppers, diced
- 1 medium (200 g/7.1 oz) zucchini, diced
- Optional: sliced avocado, shredded cheese, cilantro, lime wedges, and/or sour cream for serving

Instructions

In a large heavy-based pot greased with ghee, cook the onion over medium-high heat for 5 to 8 minutes, until lightly browned. Add the garlic and jalapeño pepper, and cook for 1 minute. Crumble in the beef and add the salt, pepper, cumin, chipotle powder, and smoked paprika. Cook over medium heat until the meat is lightly browned on all sides, stirring constantly. Add the tomato paste, tomatoes, broth, water, green peppers, and zucchini. Bring to a boil and simmer, uncovered, for about 10 minutes, or until the vegetables are tender.

Optionally, serve with avocado, shredded cheese, cilantro, lime wedges and/or sour cream. To store, let it cool, and refrigerate in an airtight container for up to 4 days or freeze for up to 3 months.

NUTRITION FACTS PER SERVING (ABOUT 1½ CUPS/360 ML):
Total carbs: 7.7 g / Fiber: 2.3 g / Net carbs: 5.4 g / Protein: 19.1 g / Fat: 25.4 g / Energy: 337 kcal
Macronutrient ratio: Calories from carbs (7%), protein (23%), fat (70%)

Autumn Oxtail Soup

Oxtail is my favorite cut of beef, and in this herb-infused, cool-weather soup, it's cooked slowly until it's so tender it falls off the bone. Paired with low-starch vegetables like rutabaga, leeks, and celery, it's an elegant, keto-friendly treat.

Ingredients

BOUQUET GARNI:

2 sprigs rosemary

2 sprigs thyme

3 bay leaves

SOUP:

¼ cup (55 g/1.9 oz) ghee or other healthy cooking fat (see page 14)

3½ pounds (1.6 kg) bone-in oxtails, will yield about 50% meat

1 teaspoon fine sea salt, or to taste

Ground black pepper

¼ teaspoon ground cloves

2 tablespoons (30ml) fresh lemon juice

8 cups (1.9 L) water

1 medium (400 g/14.1 oz) rutabaga, peeled and cut into 1-inch (2.5-cm) pieces

14.1 ounces (400 g) canned chopped tomatoes

2 cups (200 g/7.1 oz) green beans, chopped

2 medium (180 g/6.3 oz) leeks, sliced

2 medium (80 g/2.8 oz) celery stalks, sliced

Instructions

Make the bouquet garni by placing all the herbs in a piece of cheesecloth and tying with unwaxed kitchen string. This will make it easy to remove once cooked.

Heat a large pot greased with ghee over medium-high heat. Pat dry the oxtails with a paper towel and sprinkle with salt and pepper.

Place the oxtails in the pot and brown on all sides for about 10 minutes. Transfer the browned oxtails to a preheated slow cooker and add the bouquet garni, cloves, lemon juice, and water. Cook on high for 4 to 5 hours.

Add the rutabaga, tomatoes, green beans, leeks, and celery stalks in the last 2 hours of the cooking process. Once cooked, shred the meat off the bones and place it back in the soup. Discard the bones or keep them for making a batch of bone broth (page 44). Season the soup with salt and pepper to taste. To store, let it cool, and refrigerate in an airtight container for up to 4 days or freeze for up to 3 months.

NUTRITION FACTS PER SERVING (ABOUT 1½ CUPS/360 ML):
Total carbs: 9.5 g / Fiber: 2.4 g / Net carbs: 7.1 g / Protein: 26.2 g / Fat: 17.2 g / Energy: 301 kcal
Macronutrient ratio: Calories from carbs (10%), protein (36%), fat (54%)

Chapter 4

ONE-POT & SKILLET MEALS

Life gets busy and you may not always have time to cook. After a long day at work, we simply need something quick to satisfy our hunger and help us relax. Instead of reaching for unhealthy takeout, give these quick-prep keto recipes a try. From simple skillet meals—such as shakshuka and Italian sausage frittata—to comforting one-pot staples—such as gumbo and chicken jambalaya—all of these tasty meals require minimum cleanup and are convenient for every busy cook.

Pork Lo Mein

This is my take on the much-loved Chinese favorite. And, unlike the traditional version, it won't spike your insulin. What's the secret? Shirataki noodles, which are very low in carbs (and in calories). And it's packed with plenty of low-starch veggies for texture and crunch, too.

Ingredients

MARINADE:

2 tablespoons (30 ml) coconut aminos

1 tablespoon (15 ml) fish sauce

2 cloves garlic, minced

1-inch piece (6 g/0.2 oz) finely chopped ginger

STIR-FRY:

1.1 pounds (500 g) pork tenderloin, cut into thin strips

14.1 ounces (400 g) shirataki noodles, drained

¼ cup (55 g/1.9 oz) ghee or other healthy cooking fat (see page 14)

4 cups (200 g/7.1 oz) mixed Asian mushrooms (shiitake, oyster, and enoki) or brown mushrooms, sliced

½ cup (120 ml) chicken stock (page 28) or water

1 large (64 g/2.2 oz) celery stalk, sliced

1 medium (120 g/4.2 oz) green bell pepper, sliced

1 medium (120 g/4.2 oz) red bell pepper, sliced

½ cup (66 g/2.3 oz) canned bamboo shoots, drained, or fresh bean sprouts

Salt and pepper

2 tablespoons (30 ml) toasted sesame oil or extra-virgin olive oil

2 medium (30 g/1.1 oz) spring onions, sliced

Instructions

Prepare the marinade by mixing the coconut aminos, fish sauce, garlic, and ginger. Add the sliced pork, stir to combine and let it marinate for at least 30 minutes, or up to 2 hours. Prepare the shirataki noodles by following the instructions on page 19.

Grease a large skillet or Dutch oven with the ghee. Add the marinated pork and cook over medium-high heat for 3 to 5 minutes. Add the mushrooms and stock, and cook for about 5 minutes. Add the celery and peppers, and cook for 2 to 3 minutes, stirring frequently. Add the bamboo shoots and prepared shirataki noodles. Season with salt and pepper to taste. Drizzle with the sesame oil, and garnish with the spring onion. Serve immediately, or let cool and refrigerate for up to 4 days.

NUTRITION FACTS PER SERVING:
Total carbs: 12.5 g / Fiber: 4.5 g / Net carbs: 8 g / Protein: 29.3 g / Fat: 24.6 g / Energy: 381 kcal
Macronutrient ratio: Calories from carbs (9%), protein (32%), fat (59%)

Greek Briam

Briam is a traditional Greek vegetarian meal that's a distant cousin of ratatouille, and this version is proof that you don't have to go "zero-carb" to go keto: there's plenty of room in a healthy keto diet for low-starch vegetable dishes like this one!

Ingredients

¼ cup (55 g/1.9 oz) ghee or other healthy cooking fat (see page14)

1 small (70 g/2.5 oz) yellow onion, sliced

2 cloves garlic, minced

1 medium (250 g/8.8 oz) eggplant, cut into ½-inch (1-cm) pieces

½ medium (150 g/3.5 oz) broccoli, roughly chopped

½ medium (250 g/8.8 oz) cauliflower, roughly chopped

1 medium (120 g/4.2 oz) green bell pepper, sliced

3 medium (300 g/10.6 oz) tomatoes, roughly chopped

¼ cup (60 ml) water or vegetable stock (page 28)

2 small (300 g/10.6 oz) zucchini, sliced

¼ cup (15 g/0.5 oz) chopped parsley, divided

1 tablespoon freshly chopped oregano or 1 teaspoon dried oregano

¼ teaspoon fine sea salt, or to taste

Freshly ground black pepper

1½ cups (225 g/8 oz) crumbled feta cheese

½ cup (120 ml) extra-virgin olive oil

Instructions

In a large heavy-based casserole dish greased with ghee, cook the onion over medium-high heat for 5 to 8 minutes, until lightly browned. Add the garlic and eggplant, and cover with a lid. Lower the heat to medium-low and cook for 3 to 5 minutes. Add the broccoli and cauliflower, and cook, covered, for 3 to 5 minutes. Add the pepper, tomatoes, and water. Mix and cover with a lid. Cook for another 5 minutes, add the zucchini, and stir to combine. Cook, covered, for 5 to 10 minutes, or until the zucchini is tender.

Preheat the broiler. Mix in the parsley (leave some parsley for garnish), oregano, salt, and pepper. Top with the feta cheese. Place under the broiler and cook on high for about 5 minutes, or until the feta is lightly browned. Leave to cool for 5 minutes. Garnish with more parsley and drizzle with the olive oil. Eat hot or cold. Once cooled, refrigerate for up to 5 days.

NUTRITION FACTS PER SERVING:
Total carbs: 13.9 g / Fiber: 4.6 g / Net carbs: 9.3 g / Protein: 8.7 g / Fat: 35.8 g / Energy: 400 kcal
Macronutrient ratio: Calories from carbs (9%), protein (9%), fat (82%)

Green Shakshuka

Traditional shakshuka, an Arabic dish of poached eggs in tomatoes, peppers, and onions, is relatively low in carbs, but it's not suitable if you're following a strict keto diet. Luckily, it's easy to make this delicious one-skillet dish keto-friendly: just use low-carb veggies, like zucchini and spinach.

Ingredients

2 tablespoons (30 g/1.1 oz) ghee
   or other healthy cooking fat
   (see page 14)
½ small (35 g/1.2 oz) yellow
   onion, sliced
1 clove garlic, minced
1 medium (120 g/4.2 oz) green
   bell pepper, sliced
1 small (150 g/5.3 oz) zucchini,
   cut into ½-inch (1-cm) cubes
½ cup (120 g/4.2 oz) canned
   chopped tomatoes
½ teaspoon ground cumin
½ teaspoon paprika
¼ teaspoon ground coriander
⅛ teaspoon cayenne pepper
Salt and pepper
3 cups (90 g/3.2 oz) fresh
   spinach
4 large eggs
1 tablespoon (4 g/0.2 oz) freshly
   chopped cilantro or parsley
Optional: ⅓ cup (50 g/1.8 oz)
   crumbled feta cheese and
   1 medium (150 g/5.3 oz)
   avocado, sliced

Instructions

In a large skillet greased with ghee, cook the onion over medium-high heat for 5 to 8 minutes, until lightly browned.

Add the garlic, green pepper, and zucchini. Cook for about 2 minutes, stirring occasionally. Add the tomatoes, cumin, paprika, coriander, cayenne pepper, salt, and black pepper. Cook for about 5 minutes, or until the vegetables are tender.

Add the spinach and cook for a minute, until wilted.

Use a spatula to make 4 wells in the mixture. Crack 1 egg into each well and cook until the egg whites are opaque and cooked through and the egg yolks are still runny. Remove from the heat. Garnish with the cilantro, and add the optional feta cheese or avocado on top. Serve immediately, or refrigerate for up to 3 days (without the fried eggs).

NUTRITION FACTS PER SERVING:
Total carbs: 12.6 g / Fiber: 4.1 g / Net carbs: 8.5 g / Protein: 16.3 g / Fat: 25.4 g / Energy: 338 kcal
Macronutrient ratio: Calories from carbs (10%), protein (20%), fat (70%)

Egg Fried Cauli-Rice

Egg fried rice is usually a high-carb indulgence, one you'll need to avoid if you're eating low-carb. Not this version, though! Made with healthy cauli-rice (page 18), it's short on starch but big on flavor, with aromatics—like toasted sesame oil, spring onion, and garlic—that really make it sing.

Ingredients

- ¼ cup (55 g/1.9 oz) ghee or other healthy cooking fat (see page 14)
- ½ small (35 g/1.2 oz) yellow onion, sliced
- 1 clove garlic, minced
- 1 small (14 g/0.5 oz) chile pepper, sliced
- 1 medium (120 g/4.2 oz) green bell pepper, sliced
- 1 cup (70 g/2.5 oz) sliced white mushrooms
- 6 cups (720 g/1.6 lb) uncooked cauli-rice (page 18)
- 2 tablespoons (30 ml) coconut aminos
- ¼ teaspoon turmeric powder
- ¼ teaspoon paprika
- 4 large eggs, lightly beaten
- ½ teaspoon fine sea salt, or to taste
- Ground black pepper
- 2 tablespoons (30 ml) toasted sesame oil or extra-virgin olive oil
- 2 medium (30 g/1.1 oz) spring onions, sliced

Instructions

In a large skillet greased with ghee, cook the onion over medium-high heat for 5 to 8 minutes, until lightly browned. Add the garlic, chile pepper, green pepper, and mushrooms. Cook for about 5 minutes, stirring frequently. Add the prepared cauli-rice and cook for 5 to 7 minutes. Add the coconut aminos, turmeric, and paprika. In a bowl, whisk the eggs and season them with salt and pepper. Add the eggs to the skillet and continue to mix with a spatula until the eggs are cooked. Remove from the heat, drizzle with toasted sesame oil, and sprinkle with spring onion. Eat immediately or let it cool and refrigerate for up to 5 days.

NUTRITION FACTS PER SERVING:
Total carbs: 13.8 g / Fiber: 4.8 g / Net carbs: 9 g / Protein: 10.9 g / Fat: 26 g / Energy: 323 kcal
Macronutrient ratio: Calories from carbs (11%), protein (14%), fat (75%)

Halloumi Jalfrezi

Like eggplant, chunks of halloumi cheese act like little sponges when they're added to sauces; they soak up all the layers of flavor. That's why halloumi works so well in this vegetarian (and low-carb, of course!) take on jalfrezi, an Indian take-out classic.

Ingredients

⅓ cup (73 g/2.6 oz) ghee or other healthy cooking fat (see page 14), divided

1 pound (450 g) halloumi cheese, diced

1½ teaspoons whole cumin seeds

1 medium (110 g/3.9 oz) onion, sliced

2 cloves garlic, minced

1-inch piece (6 g/0.2 oz) finely chopped ginger

1 small (14 g/0.5 oz) green chile pepper, sliced

1½ teaspoons ground coriander

1½ teaspoons garam masala

½ teaspoon turmeric powder

½ teaspoon chili powder

3 medium (240 g/8.5 oz) tomatoes or 1 cup (240 g/8.5 oz) canned chopped tomatoes

½ cup (120 ml) water or vegetable stock (page 28)

1 medium (120 g/4.2 oz) red bell pepper, sliced

2 medium (240 g/8.5 oz) green bell peppers, sliced

1 medium (200 g/7.1 oz) zucchini, diced

Salt and pepper

2 tablespoons (30 ml) fresh lemon juice

Fresh cilantro or parsley for garnish

Instructions

Grease a large skillet or casserole dish with half of the ghee and heat over medium-high heat. Add the halloumi and cook until lightly browned on all sides. Use a slotted spoon to transfer the halloumi to a bowl and set aside.

Grease the pan with the remaining ghee. Add the cumin seeds and cook briefly over medium-high heat for 30 seconds. Add the onion and cook for 2 to 3 minutes, until fragrant. Add the garlic, ginger, chile pepper, coriander, garam masala, turmeric powder, and chili powder. Cook for 1 minute, stirring frequently. Add the tomatoes and vegetable stock. Cook for 1 to 2 minutes, until the sauce starts to thicken. Add the bell peppers and zucchini. Cook for 5 to 8 minutes, or until the vegetables are crisp-tender. Season with salt and pepper to taste. Take off the heat, drizzle with lemon juice, and garnish with cilantro. To store, let it cool, and refrigerate in an airtight container for up to 5 days.

NUTRITION FACTS PER SERVING:
Total carbs: 10.6 g / Fiber: 2.7 g / Net carbs: 7.9 g / Protein: 16.8 g / Fat: 33.1 g / Energy: 401 kcal
Macronutrient ratio: Calories from carbs (8%), protein (17%), fat (75%)

Quick Italian Shrimp Pasta

Since it takes just a couple of minutes to cook, protein-rich shrimp comes in handy when you needed to have dinner on the table ten minutes ago. And it's a great match for fragrant, homemade Red Pesto (page 37). Toss it with some low-carb zucchini noodles, and the job's done.

Ingredients

2 tablespoons (30 g/1.1 oz) ghee or other healthy cooking fat (see page 14)

10.6 ounces (300 g) raw, peeled shrimp

¼ cup (60 g/2.1 oz) Red Pesto (see page 37)

½ teaspoon dried oregano

Optional: ¼ teaspoon chili powder

1 tablespoon (15 ml) lemon juice

½ cup (75 g/2.7 oz) cherry tomatoes, halved

Salt and pepper

2 medium (400 g/14.1 oz) zucchini, spiralized (see page 18)

2 tablespoons (30 ml) extra-virgin olive oil

Fresh basil for garnish

Optional: 4 tablespoons (20 g/0.7 oz) grated Parmesan cheese for topping

Instructions

Grease a large skillet or casserole dish with the ghee and heat over medium-high heat. Add the shrimp and cook for 1 to 2 minutes. Add the pesto, oregano, and optional chili powder for extra heat. Cook for a minute and drizzle with the lemon juice. Add the zucchini and cook for 2 to 5 minutes, or until desired doneness. Add the tomatoes and season with salt and pepper to taste. Season with salt and pepper to taste. Just before serving, drizzle with the olive oil and garnish with fresh basil. Optionally, top with grated Parmesan cheese. For best results, always prepare fresh, or up to 1 day in advance and store in the fridge.

TIPS: If you have any leftover shrimp shells, use them to make a batch of seafood stock (page 29)! Not a fan of shrimp? Try sliced chicken thighs instead and cook them for 4 to 5 minutes before adding the pesto.

NUTRITION FACTS PER SERVING:
TOTAL CARBS: 12 g / Fiber: 3.7 g / Net carbs: 8.3 g / Protein: 25.4 g / Fat: 42.7 g / Energy: 519 kcal
MACRONUTRIENT RATIO: Calories from carbs (6%), protein (20%), fat (74%)

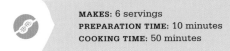
Smoked Salmon and Spinach Frittata

Frittatas aren't just for brunch; super-sophisticated versions like this one make excellent light dinners, too. If you can't find lightly smoked salmon fillets, use regular ones instead, and replace ¼ teaspoon of the salt with smoked fine sea salt, sprinkling it over the salmon fillet before using.

Ingredients

- 10 large eggs, lightly beaten
- ½ teaspoon fine sea salt
- Black pepper
- ½ cup (120 ml) heavy whipping cream
- 2 tablespoons (8 g/0.3 oz) freshly chopped chives or spring onion
- 1 tablespoon (4 g/0.2 oz) freshly chopped dill
- 2 tablespoons (30 g/1.1 oz) ghee or other healthy cooking fat (see page 14)
- 1 medium (110 g/3.9 oz) yellow onion, sliced
- 8.8 ounces (250 g) frozen spinach, thawed and drained (about 100 g/3.5 oz after draining)
- 8.8 ounces (250 g) smoked salmon fillet, skin removed and diced into 1-inch (2.5-cm) chunks
- 4.4 ounces (125 g) soft goat cheese or feta cheese, broken into chunks

Instructions

Preheat the oven to 350°F (180°C, or gas mark 4). Crack the eggs into a bowl. Season with salt and pepper, and add the cream and fresh herbs. Beat using a fork and set aside.

Grease a large ovenproof skillet or casserole dish with the ghee. Add the onion and cook over medium-high heat for 5 to 8 minutes, until lightly browned. Squeeze the excess water from the spinach and add it to the pan. Cook for just a minute to heat through. Pour in the eggs, and then add the salmon and goat cheese. Place in the oven and bake for 35 to 40 minutes, or until the top is set and lightly browned. When done, remove from the oven and set aside on a cooling rack for 5 to 10 minutes before slicing. To store, let it cool, and place in the fridge for up to 4 days or freeze for up to 3 months.

NUTRITION FACTS PER SERVING:
Total carbs: 5.2 g / Fiber: 2.1 g / Net carbs: 3.1 g / Protein: 26.1 g / Fat: 27.8 g / Energy: 378 kcal
Macronutrient ratio: Calories from carbs (3%), protein (28%), fat (69%)

One-Pot Cheese-Stuffed Meatballs

Spaghetti and meatballs just got a low-carb makeover! Here, juicy, mozzarella-stuffed meatballs are cooked in homemade marinara sauce before being tossed over fresh "zoodles," or zucchini noodles. Prepare both the meatballs and the zoodles the night before so you'll have a healthy dinner at your fingertips the next day.

Ingredients

MEATBALLS:

14.1 ounces (400 g) ground beef
½ teaspoon dried oregano
2 tablespoons (8 g/0.3 oz) freshly chopped parsley
½ teaspoon fine sea salt
¼ teaspoon ground black pepper
½ cup (45 g/1.6 oz) grated Parmesan cheese
1 egg yolk
3.5 ounces (100 g) mozzarella cheese, cut into 12 cubes
1 tablespoon (15 g/0.5 oz) ghee or other healthy cooking fat (see page 14)

SAUCE & ZOODLES:

1 recipe marinara sauce (page 25)
4 small (600 g/1.3 lb) zucchini, spiralized (see page 18)
⅓ cup (30 g/1.1 oz) grated Parmesan cheese for topping
Fresh basil or parsley for garnish

Instructions

In a bowl, mix the beef, oregano, parsley, salt, pepper, Parmesan cheese, and egg yolk. Using your hands, create 12 meatballs. Press a piece of mozzarella cheese inside each meatball and roll until enclosed completely.

Grease a large skillet or a casserole dish with the ghee and place over medium heat. Add the meatballs in a single layer, and cook for 2 minutes on each side, turning with a fork until browned on all sides and cooked through: don't turn too soon or they will crumble. Pour the prepared marinara sauce over the meatballs, bring to a boil, and cook, covered, over medium-low heat for about 10 minutes.

Add the prepared zucchini noodles and cook for 2 to 5 minutes. Sprinkle with the Parmesan cheese and garnish with fresh herbs.

If making ahead, don't add the zoodles, let it cool, and refrigerate for up to 4 days. Reheat in a pan with zoodles just before serving.

NUTRITION FACTS PER SERVING (3 MEATBALLS + SAUCE AND ZOODLES):
Total carbs: 11.1 g / Fiber: 2.7 g / Net carbs: 8.4 g / Protein: 33.8 g / Fat: 47.5 g / Energy: 605 kcal
Macronutrient ratio: Calories from carbs (6%), protein (23%), fat (71%)

Cajun Andouille Gumbo

Spicy, smoky gumbo is the official dish of the state of Louisiana, where it's usually served over rice. Replace the starchy rice with cauliflower (page 51), and you've got a big pot of low-carb comfort food at its finest.

Ingredients

- ¼ cup (55 g/1.9 oz) ghee or other healthy cooking fat (see page 14)
- 1 medium (110 g/3.9 oz) yellow onion, chopped
- 4 cloves garlic, minced
- 1 medium (120 g/4.2 oz) green bell pepper, sliced
- 2 large (128 g/4.5 oz) celery stalks, sliced
- 14.1 ounces (400 g) canned chopped tomatoes
- 4 cups (980 ml) fish stock (page 29) or chicken stock (page 28)
- 1 teaspoon dried thyme
- 1 teaspoon oregano
- 1 teaspoon ancho chile powder or smoked paprika
- ¼ teaspoon cayenne pepper
- 14.1 ounces (400 g) okra, trimmed and roughly chopped, or chopped frozen okra
- 1.1 pounds (500 g) Andouille sausages, Mexican chorizo sausages, or kielbasa, cut into 1-inch (2.5-cm) slices
- 1½ pounds (680 g) raw shrimp, peeled
- Salt and pepper
- Freshly chopped parsley, chives, or spring onions for garnish

Instructions

Grease a large heavy-based saucepan or Dutch oven with the ghee. Add the onion and cook over medium-high heat for 5 to 8 minutes, until lightly browned. Add the garlic, green pepper, and celery. Cook for 2 minutes, then add the tomatoes, stock, thyme, oregano, ancho powder, cayenne pepper, okra, and Andouille sausage. Bring to a boil, reduce the heat, and simmer, uncovered, for 25 to 30 minutes, or until the okra is tender and the gumbo has slightly thickened.

Add the shrimp and cook for 2 to 3 more minutes and then take off the heat. Season with salt and pepper to taste and garnish with fresh herbs. Serve immediately on its own, with Cauliflower Rice (page 51), or with Sourdough Keto Buns (page 52). To store, let it cool, and refrigerate for up to 4 days or freeze for up to 3 months.

TIP: If you have any leftover shrimp shells, use them to make a batch of seafood stock (page 29)! Not a fan of shrimp? Swap them for sliced chicken thighs!

NUTRITION FACTS PER SERVING:
Total carbs: 11.2 g / Fiber: 3.9 g / Net carbs: 7.3 g / Protein: 26.6 g / Fat: 22.6 g / Energy: 349 kcal
Macronutrient ratio: Calories from carbs (9%), protein (31%), fat (60%)

MAKES: 4 servings
PREPARATION TIME: 10 minutes
COOKING TIME: 35 minutes +
marinating

Filipino Chicken Adobo

This is one of my favorite one-pot wonders: Marinating chicken in rich coconut milk and Asian-inflected condiments and spices, then simmering it on the stovetop in the same marinade, yields tender meat and plenty of nuanced flavor.

Ingredients

MARINADE:

¼ cup (60 ml) coconut aminos
1 tablespoon (15 ml) fish sauce
½ cup (120 ml) coconut vinegar
or apple cider vinegar
1 cup (240 ml) coconut milk
3 bay leaves
1 teaspoon black peppercorns
4 cloves garlic, minced

CHICKEN:

4 to 6 large (800 g/1.76 lb)
bone-in chicken thighs,
trimmed of excess fat and skin
(or use 600 g/1.3 lb boneless
chicken)
Salt
1 tablespoon (15 g/0.5 oz)
coconut oil or other healthy
cooking fat (see page 14)
6 cups (720 g/1.6 lb) uncooked
cauli-rice, 1½ cups
(180 g/6.3 oz) per serving
(page 18)
2 medium (30 g/1.1 oz) spring
onions, sliced

Instructions

To make the marinade, mix the the coconut aminos, fish sauce, coconut vinegar, coconut milk, bay leaves, peppercorns, and garlic in a large bowl. Add the chicken thighs, cover, and let them marinate for 30 minutes or up to 2 hours. Remove the chicken from the marinade. Place it on a chopping board, allowing the excess marinade to drip back into the bowl. Strain the marinating liquid, discard the aromatics, and set aside. Pat dry the chicken thighs with a kitchen towel and remove any aromatics from the skin (these would burn if you leave them on). Season the skin with salt.

Heat a large skillet or casserole dish greased with the coconut oil. Once hot, add the chicken thighs in a single layer, skin-side down. Cook over medium-high heat for 5 minutes. Turn on the other side and cook for another 3 minutes. Using tongs, flip the thighs on the other side (skin-side down) and pour in the reserved marinating liquid. Bring to a boil, lower the heat to medium-low, and simmer, uncovered, for 5 to 8 minutes. Flip on the other side (skin-side up) and cook for another 15 minutes, or until the meat registers 175°F (80°C).

Transfer the chicken thighs to a plate and keep warm. Place the cauli-rice in the skillet and cook in the juices for 5 to 7 minutes, stirring frequently. Add back the chicken thighs and top with the spring onions. To store, let it cool, and refrigerate for up to 3 days.

NUTRITION FACTS PER SERVING:
Total carbs: 12.8 g / Fiber: 3.9 g / Net carbs: 8.9 g / Protein: 26.1 g / Fat: 59.4 g / Energy: 685 kcal
Macronutrient ratio: Calories from carbs (5%), protein (15%), fat (80%)

Crispy Chicken with Olives and Lemon

For a taste of summer any time of year, try this Mediterranean-style crispy chicken. It's sautéed quickly before being baked with loads of low-carb vegetables, plus sunny lemon slices, olives, capers, and plenty of herbs.

Ingredients

4 to 6 large (800 g/1.76 lb) bone-in chicken thighs, trimmed of excess fat and skin (or use 600 g/1.3 lb boneless chicken)

½ teaspoon fine sea salt, or to taste

2 tablespoons (30 g/1.1 oz) ghee or other healthy cooking fat (see page 14), divided

1 small (70 g/2.5 oz) yellow onion, sliced

3 cloves garlic, minced

⅓ cup (80 ml) water or chicken stock (page 28)

3 tablespoons (45 ml) fresh lemon juice

½ teaspoon dried thyme

½ teaspoon oregano

½ teaspoon rosemary

1 medium (400 g/14.1 oz) broccoli, cut into florets with stalks peeled and sliced

1 medium (200 g/7.1 oz) zucchini, sliced

¼ cup (35 g/1.2 oz) capers, drained

½ cup (50 g/1.8 oz) pitted olives of choice

1 whole (85 g/3 oz) lemon, sliced

Black pepper

Fresh parsley for garnish

1 tablespoon (15 ml) extra-virgin olive oil

Instructions

Season the chicken thighs with salt on all sides. Heat a large skillet or casserole dish greased with 1 tablespoon (15 g) of the ghee. Once hot, add the chicken thighs in a single layer, skin-side down. Cook over medium-high heat for 5 to 8 minutes. Turn on the other side and cook for another 3 to 5 minutes. Remove the chicken from the pan and set aside on a plate.

Preheat the oven to 375°F (190°C, or gas mark 5). Grease the skillet the remaining 1 tablespoon (15 g) ghee. Add the onion and cook for 5 to 8 minutes, until lightly browned. Add the garlic, water, lemon juice, and herbs. Add the broccoli florets and stalks. Toss them in the juices, and cook, covered, over medium-low heat for about 3 minutes. Add the zucchini, capers, olives, and browned chicken thighs. Top with lemon slices and transfer to the oven. Cook, uncovered, for 15 to 20 minutes, or until the vegetables are tender.

When done, place on a cooling rack and remove the lemon slices. Season with pepper, garnish with fresh parsley, and drizzle with olive oil. Serve immediately, or let it cool and refrigerate for up to 3 days.

NUTRITION FACTS PER SERVING:
Total carbs: 12.4 g / Fiber: 4.4 g / Net carbs: 8 g / Protein: 25.4 g / Fat: 57.9 g / Energy: 667 kcal
Macronutrient ratio: Calories from carbs (5%), protein (15%), fat (80%)

Thai Skillet Chicken

Just a few simple ingredients is all it takes to throw together this creamy, one-pot Thai curry. (Make sure you have a batch of homemade Thai Curry Paste, page 40, at the ready!) Serve it with a handful of fresh cilantro and chopped chiles for extra zing.

Ingredients

- 4 to 6 large (800 g/1.76 lb) bone-in chicken thighs, trimmed of excess fat and skin (or use 600 g/1.3 lb boneless chicken)
- Salt and pepper
- 2 tablespoons (30 g/1.1 oz) coconut oil or other healthy cooking fat (see page 14), divided
- ½ medium (56 g/2 oz) yellow onion, chopped
- 2 cloves garlic, minced
- 1 large (170 g/6 oz) green bell pepper, sliced
- 1 cup (240 ml) chicken stock (page 28) or water
- 1 cup (240 ml) coconut milk
- 1 heaping tablespoon (20 g/0.7 oz) Thai Curry Paste (page 40)
- 2 tablespoons (30 ml) fresh lime juice
- 4 cups (480 g/16.9 oz) uncooked cauli-rice (page 18)
- Optional toppings: cilantro, sliced red chile pepper, lime juice

Instructions

Season the chicken thighs with salt on all sides. Heat a large skillet or casserole dish greased with 1 tablespoon (15 g) of the coconut oil. Once hot, add the chicken thighs in a single layer, skin-side down. Cook over medium-high heat for 5 minutes. Turn on the other side and cook for another 3 minutes. Remove the chicken from the pan and set aside on a plate.

Grease the pan with the remaining 1 tablespoon (15 g) ghee. Add the onion and garlic and cook for 2 to 3 minutes, until fragrant. Add the green pepper and cook for another minute. Pour in the chicken stock and coconut milk. Add the curry paste and lime juice. Season with salt and pepper to taste.

Place the chicken, skin-side up, back in the pan and cook for 10 to 12 minutes. Place the pan under a broiler to crisp up for 3 to 5 minutes. Remove from the oven and let it cool for 5 minutes. Cook the cauli-rice in the meat juices for 5 to 7 minutes before serving. Optionally, garnish with cilantro, chile peppers, and lime juice. To store, let it cool, and refrigerate for up to 3 days.

NUTRITION FACTS PER SERVING:
Total carbs: 12.7 g / Fiber: 3.6 g / Net carbs: 9.1 g / Protein: 26.5 g / Fat: 64.3 g / Energy: 725 kcal
Macronutrient ratio: Calories from carbs (5%), protein (15%), fat (80%)

Chicken & Chorizo Jambalaya

A staple of Creole cuisine, jambalaya is a spiced, stick-to-your-ribs dish that's usually rice-based—but my (healthier!) version is firmly keto-friendly. It works well with both chicken and shrimp, so feel free to substitute one for the other.

Ingredients

- 2 tablespoons (30 g/1.1 oz) ghee or other healthy cooking fat (see page 14), divided
- 1 pound (450 g) boneless and skinless chicken thighs, sliced
- 1 small (70 g/2.5 oz) yellow onion, sliced
- 1 small (14 g/0.5 oz) red chile pepper, chopped
- 2 cloves garlic, minced
- 4.5 ounces (128 g) Spanish chorizo sausage or pepperoni
- 1 medium (120 g/4.2 oz) red bell pepper, sliced
- 1 tablespoon (7 g/0.3 oz) Cajun seasoning (make your own, page 22)
- ¼ cup (60 ml) chicken stock (page 28) or water
- 4 cups (480 g/16.9 oz) uncooked cauli-rice (page 18)
- 4 cups (120 g/4.2 oz) fresh spinach
- Salt
- 4 tablespoons (60 ml) extra-virgin olive oil

Instructions

Grease a large skillet or casserole dish with 1 tablespoon (15 g) of the ghee. Add the chicken and cook for 5 to 8 minutes, until browned on all sides. Transfer to a plate and set aside.

Grease the skillet with the remaining 1 tablespoon (15 g) ghee, add onion and cook over medium-high heat for 5 to 8 minutes, until lightly browned. Add the chile pepper, garlic, chorizo, and red pepper. Cook for about 5 minutes. Add back the chicken, Cajun seasoning, stock, and cauli-rice. Cook for 5 to 7 minutes, stirring frequently. Add the spinach and cook until wilted, about 1 minute. Season with salt to taste and drizzle with the olive oil. Serve immediately, or let it cool and refrigerate for up to 5 days.

NUTRITION FACTS PER SERVING:
Total carbs: 13.1 g / Fiber: 4.8 g / Net carbs: 8.3 g / Protein: 33.8 g / Fat: 39.2 g / Energy: 536 kcal
Macronutrient ratio: Calories from carbs (6%), protein (26%), fat (68%)

Coq Au Vin

This is my low-carb version of the well-loved French classic: I just can't say no to tender chicken cooked in fragrant spices, vegetables, and rich Burgundy wine.

Ingredients

BOUQUET GARNI:

4 bay leaves
4 thyme sprigs
1 teaspoon black peppercorns
Small bunch parsley

CHICKEN:

6 large (180 g/6.4 oz) slices bacon, chopped
8 large (1.6 kg/3.5 lb) bone-in chicken thighs, trimmed of excess fat and skin (or use 1.2 kg/2.7 lb boneless chicken)
Sea salt and ground black pepper to taste
2 tablespoons (30 g/1.1 oz) ghee or other healthy cooking fat (see page 14), divided
5.3 ounces (150 g) baby onions, peeled
2 large (128 g/4.5 oz) celery stalks, sliced
2 cloves garlic, minced
4 cups (300 g/10.6 oz) sliced white mushrooms
1 bottle (750 ml) dry red wine (see page 31 for substitutions)
1 cup (250 ml) water or chicken stock (page 28)
2 tablespoons (30 g/1.1 oz) unsweetened tomato paste
Fresh parsley for garnish

Instructions

Make the bouquet garni by placing all the herbs in a piece of cheesecloth and tying with unwaxed kitchen string.

Place the bacon slices in a large pan and add ½ cup (120 ml) of water. Cook over medium-high heat until the water starts to boil. Reduce the heat to medium and cook for about 10 minutes, until the water evaporates and the bacon is crisped up. Use a slotted spoon to transfer the bacon to a plate and set aside.

Season the chicken thighs with salt on all sides. Grease the casserole dish where you cooked the bacon with half of the ghee, and add the chicken thighs in a single layer, skin-side down. Cook over medium-high heat for 5 to 8 minutes. Turn on the other side and cook for another 3 minutes. Remove the chicken from the pan and set aside on a plate.

Grease the casserole dish with the remaining ghee and add the whole onions. Cook for 5 to 8 minutes, turning occasionally. Add the celery, garlic, and mushrooms, and cook for 1 minute. Pour in the wine and bring to a boil, scraping the browned bits from the bottom of the pan with a spatula. Add the water, tomato paste, and bouquet garni. Mix until combined, and season with salt and pepper.

Place the chicken, skin-side up, back in the pan and spoon the pan juices over the chicken. Cover with a lid and cook for 25 to 30 minutes. Add the crisped-up bacon and stir in the sauce. Place the casserole dish under a broiler to crisp up for about 5 minutes. Remove from the oven and let it cool for a few minutes. Serve with cauliflower mash (page 48) or steamed low-carb veggies (page 21). To store, let it cool, and refrigerate for up to 3 days.

NUTRITION FACTS PER SERVING:
Total carbs: 6.4 g / Fiber: 1.1 g / Net carbs: 5.3 g / Protein: 25.8 g / Fat: 50.8 g / Energy: 653 kcal
Macronutrient ratio: Calories from carbs (4%), protein (17%), fat (79%)

Thai Pork Lettuce Cups

This recipe's a savior when it comes to super-busy weeknights. Just stir-fry minced pork with homemade curry paste and a couple of Thai-style condiments, then spoon the mixture into lettuce cups for a fuss-free meal. It's ready in less than half an hour, and, better yet, keeps cleanup to a bare minimum.

Ingredients

1 tablespoon (15 g/0.5 oz) ghee or other healthy cooking fat (see page 14)

3 medium (45 g/1.6 oz) spring onions, white and green parts separated and sliced

3 tablespoons (45 g/1.6 oz) Thai Curry Paste (page 40)

1.3 pounds (600 g) ground pork, 20% fat

2 tablespoons (30 ml/1 oz.) fish sauce

4 cups (480 g/16.9 oz) uncooked cauli-rice (page 18)

½ cup (120 ml) coconut milk

1 tablespoon (15 ml/10.5 oz) fresh lime juice

Salt and pepper

1 head (400 g/14.1 oz) iceberg lettuce or any green lettuce

1 tablespoon (15 ml/0.5 oz) olive oil

Instructions

In a large heavy-based pot greased with ghee, cook the white part of the onion over medium heat for 2 to 3 minutes, stirring frequently. Add the curry paste and pork and cook until browned on all sides, 3 to 5 minutes. Add the fish sauce, cauli-rice, coconut milk, and lime juice. Cook, uncovered, for an additional 7 to 8 minutes, stirring frequently. Season with salt and pepper to taste. Remove from the heat and mix in the green parts of the spring onions. Spoon the pork mixture on top of lettuce leaves, drizzle with the olive oil, and serve. The cooked pork can be stored in the fridge for up to 4 days.

NUTRITION FACTS PER SERVING:
Total carbs: 13.1 g / Fiber: 4.2 g / Net carbs: 8.8 g / Protein: 30.1 g / Fat: 42.1 g / Energy: 545 kcal
Macronutrient ratio: Calories from carbs (6%), protein (21%), fat (73%)

MAKES: 4 servings
PREPARATION TIME: 15 minutes
COOKING TIME: 30 minutes

Italian Sausage Frittata

So easy they're practically foolproof, frittatas are the ultimate one-dish meal. This one's especially big on flavor, thanks to savory Italian sausage, two kinds of cheese, and plenty of low-carb veggies. Make it ahead of time and enjoy it tomorrow—if you can keep your hands off it tonight, that is.

Ingredients

- 2 tablespoons (30 g/1.1 oz) ghee or other healthy cooking fat (see page 14)
- 7.1 ounces (200 g) gluten-free Italian-style sausages
- 2 medium (30 g/1.1 oz) spring onions, white and green parts sliced and separated
- 1 medium (120 g/4.2 oz) red bell pepper, sliced
- 2 cloves garlic, minced
- 4 ounces (112 g) Swiss chard, stalks and leaves separated and roughly chopped
- 8 large eggs
- 1 teaspoon dried Italian herbs
- ¼ teaspoon fine sea salt
- Ground black pepper
- 1 cup (113 g/4 oz) grated mozzarella cheese, divided
- ½ cup (45 g/1.6 oz) grated Parmesan cheese, divided
- ½ cup (75 g/2.7 oz) cherry tomatoes, halved

Instructions

Grease a large skillet with the ghee. Add the sausages and cook over medium-low heat for 10 to 12 minutes, until browned on all sides and cooked through. Transfer to a plate and set aside. Let them cool slightly and then cut into about 1-inch (2.5-cm) pieces.

Place the white parts of the spring onions in the skillet where you cooked the sausages and cook for 2 to 3 minutes, stirring frequently. Add the red pepper, garlic, and chard stalks. Cook for 3 minutes, stirring frequently. Add the chard leaves and cook for 1 minute.

Preheat the broiler. Lightly beat the eggs with the herbs, salt, and pepper. Add the mozzarella and Parmesan cheese (reserve some cheese for topping). Pour the eggs into the skillet. Cook over low heat until the top starts to firm up and the edges are turning opaque, 8 to 10 minutes. Top with the reserved cheese, browned sausages, cherry tomatoes, and green parts of the spring onions. Place under the broiler for about 5 minutes to crisp up the top. Let the frittata cool slightly and cut it into 4 pieces. Serve immediately or let it cool and refrigerate for up to 4 days, or freeze for up to 3 months.

NUTRITION FACTS PER SERVING (¼ FRITTATA):
Total carbs: 7.4 g / Fiber: 1.9 g / Net carbs: 5.5 g / Protein: 33.4 g / Fat: 34.7 g / Energy: 479 kcal
Macronutrient ratio: Calories from carbs (5%), protein (28%), fat (67%)

Chapter 5

SAVORY STEWS, ROASTS & CASSEROLES

Stews, roasts, and casseroles are really convenient because you can cook affordable meat cuts in bulk, freeze, and enjoy them later. All you have to do is prepare the ingredients, throw them in a slow cooker, and let it do its magic. When a comforting stew is ready when you get back from work, everything gets better. To make defrosting and reheating easy, freeze the dishes in appropriate-sized containers or freezer bags.

This chapter features all-time favorites from all over the world. All of these dishes have something else in common: they require minimal prep time! You can now enjoy several European classics, including osso buco, moussaka, and Irish lamb shanks. There's even more for those who love Indian curries, African tagines, or American favorites, including beef short ribs, pulled pork sliders, and beef tacos. These recipes will help you cook crowd-pleasing dishes that are easy to prepare and packed with flavor. This means you can spend less time in the kitchen and more time with your family and friends.

Green Bean Casserole

No Thanksgiving dinner is complete without a creamy, cheesy, onion-flecked green bean casserole! And there's a good reason that this twentieth-century classic is such a festive favorite: it's the perfect accompaniment for roast turkey.

Ingredients

- 1½ pounds (680 g) green beans, trimmed
- 2 tablespoons (30 g/1.1 oz) ghee or other healthy cooking fat (see page 14)
- 1 medium (110 g/3.9 oz) yellow onion, sliced
- 1 cup (240 ml) heavy whipping cream
- 1 cup (240 g/8.5 oz) full-fat cream cheese
- 2 cloves garlic, minced
- 4 cups (280 g/9.9 oz) sliced white mushrooms
- Salt and pepper

Instructions

Preheat the oven to 350°F (175°C, or gas mark 4). Bring a large saucepan filled with salted water to a boil and blanch the green beans for just about a minute, until they turn bright green. Drain and rinse them in cold water. Transfer the greens to a bowl and set aside.

In a large skillet or a casserole dish greased with the ghee, cook the onion over medium-high heat for 2 to 3 minutes, until fragrant. Add them to the bowl with the green beans. In the same pan where you cooked the onion, whisk the cream with the cream cheese and garlic. Cook for about 5 minutes, and then add the mushrooms. Simmer for 5 to 7 minutes, and then add the green beans with fried onion. Combine using a spatula. Season with salt and pepper.

Transfer the skillet to the oven and bake for 25 to 30 minutes, until the green beans are tender. Serve immediately as a side with meat or a light dish, or let it cool and store in an airtight container in the fridge for up to 5 days.

NUTRITION FACTS PER SERVING:
Total carbs: 10.3 g / Fiber: 3 g / Net carbs: 7.3 g / Protein: 5.5 g / Fat: 23.9 g / Energy: 257 kcal
Macronutrient ratio: Calories from carbs (11%), protein (8%), fat (81%)

Cheesy Cauliflower Casserole

MAKES: 8 servings
PREPARATION TIME: 15 minutes
COOKING TIME: 35 minutes

With just a handful of pantry ingredients, this hearty vegetarian casserole is the perfect solution when you're short on time. It's got plenty of low-carb, fiber-rich vegetables like broccolini and asparagus, but it gets its (serious) heft from protein-packed eggs and cheese.

Ingredients

- ¼ cup (55 g/1.9 oz) ghee or other healthy cooking fat (see page 14)
- 1 small (70 g/2.5 oz) yellow onion, chopped
- 5.3 ounces (150 g) broccolini or broccoli, cut into florets
- 5.3 ounces (150 g) asparagus, cut into thirds
- 1 large cauliflower (1 kg/2.2 lb), riced (page 18)
- ¼ cup (60 g/2.1 oz) Red Pesto (page 37)
- ½ cup (120 g/4.2 oz) canned chopped tomatoes
- Salt and pepper
- 2 cups (226 g/8 oz) shredded cheese of choice (Cheddar, Manchego, Gouda, or Gruyère), divided
- 6 large eggs, lightly beaten

Instructions

Preheat the oven to 360°F (180°C, or gas mark 4). In a large skillet greased with the ghee, cook the onion over medium-high heat for 5 to 8 minutes, until lightly browned. Add the broccolini and asparagus, and cook for 2 to 3 minutes. Add the cauliflower rice and cook for about 5 minutes, stirring frequently.

Add the pesto and tomatoes, and cook for 2 to 3 minutes. Season with salt and pepper to taste. Add the shredded cheese (reserve some for topping) and combine with the ingredients. Take off the heat, pour in the beaten eggs, and stir to combine. Top with the reserved cheese and transfer to the oven. Bake for 15 to 18 minutes, or until the top is lightly browned and crispy.

When done, let it cool for a few minutes before slicing and serving. To store, let it cool, and refrigerate for up to 5 days or freeze for up to 3 months.

NUTRITION FACTS PER SERVING:
Total carbs: 11.1 g / Fiber: 4 g / Net carbs: 7.1 g / Protein: 15.6 g / Fat: 23.3 g / Energy: 308 kcal
Macronutrient ratio: Calories from carbs (9%), protein (21%), fat (70%)

Broccoli & Mushroom Alfredo Casserole

Since it's so rich and comforting, this quick-prep dish is another holiday classic, but you don't have to wait for winter to enjoy it. Make it in advance as part of an easy midweek dinner at any time of year.

Ingredients

- 2 large (800 g/1.8 lbs) broccoli
- ¼ cup (55 g/1.9 oz) ghee or other healthy cooking fat (see page 14)
- 1 small (70 g/2.5 oz) yellow onion, chopped
- 1 cup (240 ml) heavy whipping cream
- 2 cloves garlic, minced
- 1 teaspoon dried Italian herbs
- 3 cups (210 g/7.4 oz) sliced white or brown mushrooms
- 1½ cups (135 g/4.8 oz) grated Parmesan cheese, divided
- Salt and pepper

Instructions

Preheat the oven to 360°F (180°C, or gas mark 4). Cut the broccoli into florets. Peel and chop the broccoli stalks. Bring a saucepan filled with salted water to a boil. Add the broccoli and cook for 3 to 4 minutes, until crisp-tender. Drain and set aside to let any excess water drip.

Grease a large skillet or casserole dish with the ghee. Add the onion and cook over medium-high heat for 5 to 8 minutes, until lightly browned. Pour in the cream, garlic, and Italian herbs. Bring to a boil and add the mushrooms. Cook, uncovered, for 5 to 7 minutes, and add the Parmesan cheese (reserve some for topping) and blanched broccoli. Taste and season with salt and pepper.

Take off the heat and top with the reserved Parmesan cheese. Transfer to the oven and bake for 25 to 30 minutes, or until crisped up and lightly browned. Serve immediately, or let it cool and place in an airtight container. Refrigerate for up to 5 days.

NUTRITION FACTS PER SERVING:
Total carbs: 13.2 g / Fiber: 4.1 g / Net carbs: 9.1 g / Protein: 13.8 g / Fat: 30.8 g / Energy: 377 kcal
Macronutrient ratio: Calories from carbs (10%), protein (15%), fat (75%)

MAKES: 8 servings
PREPARATION TIME: 15 minutes
COOKING TIME: 3 hours

Slow Cooker Green Frittata

This recipe is proof that anything can be made in a slow cooker—even a frittata! The trick is to place a piece of highly-absorbent paper towel on top of the bowl in order to soak up any excess moisture.

Ingredients

- ¼ cup (55 g/1.9 oz) ghee or other healthy cooking fat (see page 14), divided
- 1 medium (110 g/3.9 oz) yellow onion, chopped
- 4 cloves garlic, minced
- 14.1 ounces (400 g) dark-leaf kale, chopped and tough stalks removed
- ½ cup (120 g/4.2 oz) Red Pesto (page 37)
- 16 large eggs
- 1 teaspoon fine sea salt
- ¼ teaspoon black pepper
- 2 teaspoons dried Italian herbs
- 2 tablespoons (8 g/0.3 oz) freshly chopped parsley
- 8.8 ounces (250 g) soft goat cheese or feta cheese
- Optional: hot sauce for serving

Instructions

Preheat a 5- to 6-quart (4.7- to 5.7-L) slow cooker and grease the bowl with 1 tablespoon (15 g) of the ghee. Grease a large skillet or casserole dish with the remaining 3 tablespoons (40 g) ghee. Add the onion and cook over medium-high heat for 5 to 8 minutes, until lightly browned. Reduce the heat to medium and add the garlic and kale. Cook for about 5 minutes, stirring occasionally. Transfer everything to the slow cooker. Add the pesto and toss until the kale is coated on all sides.

Crack the eggs into a bowl and season with the salt and pepper. Add the Italian herbs and the parsley. Lightly beat with a fork and pour over the kale in the slow cooker, then add chunks of goat cheese. Place 2 layers of high-absorbent paper towels or a tea towel on top of the ceramic bowl and cover with a lid (see tips for reduced condensation, page 12). Cook on low for 3 hours. Optionally, top with hot sauce before serving. To store, let it cool, and refrigerate for up to 5 days or freeze for up to 3 months.

NUTRITION FACTS PER SERVING:
Total carbs: 7.5 g / Fiber: 2.5 g / Net carbs: 5 g / Protein: 21.1 g / Fat: 30 g / Energy: 378 kcal
Macronutrient ratio: Calories from carbs (5%), protein (23%), fat (72%)

Slow Cooker Eggplant Parmesan

Eggplant parm is usually off-menu on a low-carb lifestyle, because the eggplant slices are often doused in breadcrumbs. Not in this version, though! Whether you follow a vegetarian keto diet year-round or just don't feel like eating meat tonight, you can feel free to indulge in this filling, flavorful, keto-friendly casserole.

Ingredients

- 2 tablespoons (30 g/1.1 oz) ghee or other healthy cooking fat (see page 14)
- 3 medium (1 kg/2.2 lb) eggplants
- Salt and ground black pepper
- 1 recipe marinara sauce (page 25)
- 2 cups (480 g/16.9 oz) full-fat ricotta cheese
- 2 cups (226 g/8 oz) shredded mozzarella cheese, divided
- 1 cup (90 g/3.2 oz) grated Parmesan cheese, divided
- ¼ cup (60 ml) extra-virgin olive oil
- Fresh basil for garnish

Instructions

Preheat a 5- to 6-quart (4.7- to 5.7-L) slow cooker and grease it with the ghee. Using a sharp knife, slice the eggplant width-wise into thin ¼-inch (½-cm) slices. Season with salt on both sides and set aside for 20 minutes. Use a paper towel to pat dry any excess moisture.

In the meantime, mix the marinara sauce, ricotta cheese, mozzarella, and Parmesan (reserve some mozzarella and Parmesan for topping). Mix and season with salt and pepper to taste.

Place the first layer of the eggplant slices in the slow cooker. Top with half of the cheese mixture. Add another eggplant layer, a cheese layer, and finally the last eggplant layer. Top with the reserved cheese. Place 2 layers of high-absorbent paper towels or a tea towel on top of the ceramic bowl and cover with a lid (see tips for reduced condensation, page 12). Cook on high for 4 hours or on low for 8 hours. To serve, drizzle with the olive oil and garnish with fresh basil leaves. To store, let it cool, and refrigerate for up to 5 days, freeze for up to 3 months.

NUTRITION FACTS PER SERVING:
Total carbs: 12.8 g / Fiber: 4.3 g / Net carbs: 8.5 g / Protein: 19.8 g / Fat: 33.2 g / Energy: 422 kcal
Macronutrient ratio: Calories from carbs (8%), protein (19%), fat (73%)

Spanish Omelet

I love rustic Spanish omelets, and I really missed them when I first started following a low-carb lifestyle, so I came up with my own low-carb take on the tapas-bar staple using rutabaga in place of starchy potatoes.

Ingredients

- ⅓ cup (73 g/2.6 oz) ghee or other healthy cooking fat (see page 14), divided
- 1 large (600 g/1.3 lb) rutabaga, cut into ¼-inch (½-cm) slices
- ¾ teaspoon fine sea salt, or to taste
- ¼ teaspoon black pepper
- 1 small (70 g/2.5 oz) yellow onion, sliced
- 1 medium (120 g/4.2 oz) red bell pepper, sliced
- 8 large eggs
- 1 medium (15 g/0.5 oz) spring onion, sliced

Instructions

Preheat and grease the slow cooker with 1 tablespoon (15 g) of the ghee, and place a layer of rutabaga slices inside. Season with salt and pepper, and drizzle with another 1 tablespoon (15 g) of ghee. Add another layer of rutabaga slices, season with salt, and drizzle with the remaining ghee. Place 2 layers of high-absorbent paper towels or a tea towel on top of the ceramic bowl and cover with a lid (see tips for reduced condensation on page 12). Cook on low for 2 hours.

Grease a skillet with the remaining ghee. Add the onion and cook over medium-high heat for 5 to 8 minutes. Add the red pepper slices. Cook for 2 minutes, take off the heat, and set aside.

Whisk the eggs in a bowl, and season them with salt and pepper. Add the fried onion and pepper, and stir to combine. After 2 hours of cooking, remove the paper towel and pour the egg mixture inside. Use a spoon to allow the eggs to soak between the rutabaga slices. Cook for another hour, or until the eggs are set and the rutabaga is tender. To serve, slice the omelet and sprinkle with fresh spring onion. To store, let it cool, and refrigerate for up to 5 days or freeze for up to 3 months.

NUTRITION FACTS PER SERVING:
Total carbs: 12.1 g / Fiber: 3.2 g / Net carbs: 8.9 g / Protein: 9.9 g / Fat: 18.8 g / Energy: 257 kcal
Macronutrient ratio: Calories from carbs (15%), protein (16%), fat (69%)

Sardine Bouillabaisse

I can't think of a good reason not to eat sardines. They're protein-rich and high in omega-3 fats; they're budget-friendly; and they're relatively sustainable, so they're an environmentally sound choice. And they shine in this simple, low-carb take on bouillabaisse, the tomato-based Provençal fish stew.

Ingredients

BOUQUET GARNI:

3 sprigs thyme

3 sprigs parsley

3 bay leaves

1 teaspoon black peppercorns

STEW:

2 tablespoons (30 g/1.1 oz) ghee or other healthy cooking fat (see page 14)

1 small (60 g/2.1 oz) red onion, sliced

3 cloves garlic, minced

1 cup (240 g/8.8 oz) canned chopped tomatoes

2 cups (480 ml) fish stock (page 29) or chicken stock (page 28)

1 medium (200 g/7.1 oz) fennel bulb, sliced

1 large (500 g/1.1 lb) rutabaga, cut into ¼-inch (½-cm) slices

½ teaspoon fine sea salt, or to taste

Ground black pepper

2 pounds (900 g) frozen deboned sardines, thawed

½ cup (120 ml) extra-virgin olive oil

Fresh thyme or parsley for garnish

Instructions

Make the bouquet garni by placing all the herbs in a piece of cheesecloth and tying with unwaxed kitchen string.

Preheat the oven to 300°F (150°C, or gas mark 2). Grease a large casserole dish or Dutch oven with the ghee. Add the onion and cook over medium-high heat for 5 to 8 minutes, until lightly browned. Add the garlic and cook for a minute. Add the tomatoes, fish stock, bouquet garni, fennel, rutabaga, salt, and pepper. Bring to a boil. Cover with a lid, transfer to the oven, and cook for 25 to 30 minutes.

After 30 minutes, top the vegetables with the sardines, increase the heat to 350°F (175°C, or gas mark 4), and cook, uncovered, for 20 to 25 minutes. When done, remove from the oven and set aside for 5 minutes. Drizzle with the olive oil, garnish with the fresh herbs, and serve. To store, let it cool, and refrigerate for up to 4 days.

NUTRITION FACTS PER SERVING:
Total carbs: 13.2 g / Fiber: 4 g / Net carbs: 9.2 g / Protein: 32.9 g / Fat: 34.2 g / Energy: 456 kcal
Macronutrient ratio: Calories from carbs (8%), protein (28%), fat (64%)

Fish Ball Tagine with Harissa

Packed with aromatics like garlic, cumin, and harissa, this Tunisian favorite is perfect with cauliflower rice to help soak up its rich sauce. Like the Make-Ahead Freezer Meatballs on page 45, these fish balls can be prepared in advance and frozen—then just add them to the freshly made sauce.

Ingredients

FISH BALLS:

1 small (70 g/2.5 oz) yellow onion, roughly chopped

2 cloves garlic, sliced

1 teaspoon ground cumin

2 tablespoons (30 g/1.1 oz) mild Harissa Paste (page 39)

½ teaspoon fine sea salt, or to taste

Ground black pepper

1.1 pounds (500 g) white fish (such as cod or haddock), skinless, boneless, and cut into chunks

1 large egg

¼ cup (30 g/1.1 oz) coconut flour

1 tablespoon (4 g/0.2 oz) chopped cilantro

1 tablespoon (4 g/0.2 oz) parsley

¼ cup (55 g/1.9 oz) ghee or other healthy cooking fat (see page 14)

Instructions

Preheat the slow cooker. Place all the aromatics for the fish balls in a food processor: onion, garlic, cumin, harissa paste, salt, and pepper to taste. Process until smooth, and add the fish. Pulse until well combined. Place the fish mixture in a bowl and combine with the egg, coconut flour, and fresh herbs. Using your hands, create 20 fish balls (each about 35 g/1.2 oz) and set aside.

To brown the fish balls, heat a large skillet greased with the ghee and cook the fish balls over medium-high heat for 2 minutes on each side, turning with a fork until browned on all sides and cooked through. (Don't turn too soon or they will crumble.) Transfer the fish balls to the slow cooker.

For the sacue, add the harissa, garlic, tomatoes, stock, and coconut butter to the pan where you browned the fish balls. Season with salt and pepper to taste. Bring to a boil and mix until the coconut butter is dissolved. Then pour into the slow cooker over the fish balls. Cover with a lid and cook on low for 2 to 3 hours.

When done, garnish with fresh herbs. Serve with plain or flavored cauliflower rice (page 51). To store, let it cool, and keep in an airtight container in the fridge for up to 4 days or freeze for up to 3 months.

NUTRITION FACTS PER SERVING (5 FISH BALLS):
Total carbs: 11.2 g / Fiber: 4.4 g / Net carbs: 6.8 g / Protein: 28.2 g / Fat: 24.2 g / Energy: 378 kcal
Macronutrient ratio: Calories from carbs (8%), protein (32%), fat (60%)

SAUCE:

1 tablespoon (15 g/0.5 oz) mild
Harissa Paste (page 39)

1 clove garlic, minced

1 cup (240 g/8.5 oz) chopped
canned tomatoes

1 cup (240 ml) chicken stock
(page 28) or fish stock
(page 29)

2 tablespoons (32 g/1.1 oz)
coconut butter or almond
butter

Salt and pepper

Freshly chopped parsley or
cilantro for garnish

Suggested side: cauli-rice (page
18) or shirataki rice (page 19)

TIPS: Using a tagine dish? Preheat the oven to 350°F (175°C, or gas mark 4). Prepare the sauce with an additional ½ cup (120 ml) stock or water and pour into the tagine dish. Add the fish balls, cover with a lid, and bake for 20 to 25 minutes.

Using a skillet? Add ½ cup (120 ml) stock or water and cook the fish balls in the sauce over medium heat for 10 to 15 minutes.

Just like the Make-Ahead Freezer Meatballs (page 45), these fish balls can be prepared ahead of time and freeze for up to 3 months.

Fish & Seafood Bouillabaisse

This nutrient-dense fish stew is full of chunky, low-carb vegetables plus a mixture of seafood, and it gets its subtle flavor from fragrant herbs and a pinch of golden saffron. Top a bowl with a dollop of homemade aioli for an extra dose of healthy fats.

Ingredients

STEW:

¼ cup (55 g/1.9 oz) ghee or other healthy cooking fat (see page 14)

1 small (70 g/2.5 oz) yellow onion, chopped

1 clove garlic, minced

3 large (192 g/6.8 oz) celery stalks, sliced

1 cup (240 g/8.5 oz) canned chopped tomatoes

2 cups (480 ml) seafood stock, fish stock (page 29) or water

2 tablespoons (30 ml) fresh lemon juice

2 teaspoons dried oregano

1 teaspoon dried thyme

½ teaspoon red pepper flakes

Pinch of saffron

½ medium (300 g/10.6 oz) cauliflower, cut into florets

7.1 ounces (200 g) dark-leaf kale, chopped and stems removed

7.1 ounces (200 g) baby turnips, halved, or 1 medium turnip, diced

¾ teaspoon fine sea salt, or to taste

Ground black pepper

2 large (300 g/10.6 oz) salmon fillets, skinless, cut into large 1½-inch (4-cm) cubes

¾ pound (340 g) raw shrimp, peeled

½ pound (225 g) cooked mixed seafood of choice (mussels, clams, squid)

¼ cup (15 g/0.5 oz) freshly chopped parsley, divided

AIOLI:

¾ cup (110 g/3.9 oz) mayonnaise (page 25)

3 cloves garlic, minced

Salt and pepper

Instructions

Grease a large casserole dish or Dutch oven with the ghee. Add the onion and cook over medium-high heat for 5 to 8 minutes, until lightly browned. Add the garlic and cook for a minute. Add the celery, tomatoes, seafood stock, lemon juice, oregano, thyme, pepper flakes, saffron, cauliflower florets, kale, and turnips. Season with salt and pepper to taste. Bring to a boil and cook for 8 to 10 minutes, or until the vegetables are tender.

Add the salmon, cover with a lid, and cook for 2 to 3 minutes. Add the shrimp and cook, covered, for another 2 to 3 minutes. Finally, add the cooked seafood and half of the parsley, and heat through. Take off the heat and let it sit for 5 minutes.

Prepare the aioli by mixing the mayonnaise and garlic. Season with salt and pepper to taste. Serve the stew with the prepared aioli and garnish with the remaining parsley. To store, let it cool, and refrigerate for up to 3 days.

NUTRITION FACTS PER SERVING:
Total carbs: 13.8 g / Fiber: 4.7 g / Net carbs: 9.1 g / Protein: 29.1 g / Fat: 37.1 g / Energy: 496 kcal
Macronutrient ratio: Calories from carbs (7%), protein (24%), fat (69%)

Poached Salmon With Lemon & Dill

If you're feeling pared-down and minimalist, all you want for dinner is a delicate, gently cooked piece of salmon. Just pop your salmon fillets into the slow cooker with rutabaga, fresh herbs, lemon juice, and a little cream, and they'll turn out tender and juicy every time.

Ingredients

- 3 tablespoons (45 ml) ghee or other healthy cooking fat (see page 14), melted, divided
- 1 large (500 g/1.1 lb) rutabaga, peeled and cut into ¼-inch (½-cm) slices
- ½ teaspoon fine sea salt, or to taste
- Ground black pepper
- 2 tablespoons (30 ml) water or fish stock (page 29)
- 4 medium (150 g/5.3 oz each) salmon fillets
- 2 tablespoons (8 g/0.3 oz) chopped dill
- 2 tablespoons (30 ml) fresh lemon juice
- ¼ cup (60 ml) heavy whipping cream or coconut milk
- 4 tablespoons (60 ml) extra-virgin olive oil

Instructions

Preheat and grease the slow cooker with 1 tablespoon (15 g) of the ghee and place a layer of rutabaga slices inside. Season with salt and pepper and drizzle with another 1 tablespoon (15 g) of ghee. Add another layer of rutabaga slices, season with salt, and drizzle with the remaining 1 tablespoon (15 g) ghee, and add the water. Place 2 layers of high-absorbent paper towels or a tea towel on top of the ceramic bowl and cover with a lid (see tips for reduced condensation, page 12). Cook on low for 2 hours.

Add the salmon fillets, season with salt and pepper, add the dill, and drizzle with the lemon juice. Cook for another 1 to 2 hours. (The exact time will vary based on the thickness of the fillets and how done you prefer the salmon to be. Check the salmon after an hour and then every 20 to 30 minutes.) Add the heavy whipping cream in the last 30 minutes of the cooking process. To serve, drizzle with 1 tablespoon (15 ml) olive oil per serving. To store, place in an airtight container, and refrigerate for up to 3 days.

NUTRITION FACTS PER SERVING:
Total carbs: 11.8 g / Fiber: 3 g / Net carbs: 8.8 g / Protein: 34.2 g / Fat: 39.6 g / Energy: 544 kcal
Macronutrient ratio: Calories from carbs (7%), protein (26%), fat (67%)

Ranch Chicken Casserole

MAKES: 6 servings
PREPARATION TIME: 20 minutes
COOKING TIME: 35 minutes

Starving? Never fear: twenty minutes is all it takes to pull together this hunger-slaying—and highly kid-friendly!—casserole. Just slather chicken and low-carb veggies in a two-ingredient homemade ranch dressing plus a snowstorm of Cheddar cheese, bake, and dinner is served.

Ingredients

- 1 tablespoon (7 g/0.3 oz) ranch seasoning (make your own, page 22)
- 1 cup (230 g/8.1 oz) full-fat sour cream
- 1 small (400 g/14.1 oz) cauliflower, cut into florets
- 1 medium (300 g/10.6 oz) broccoli, cut into florets
- 2 tablespoons (30 g/1.1 oz) ghee or other healthy cooking fat (see page 14)
- 1.3 pounds (600 g) boneless and skinless chicken thighs, sliced
- 1 medium (120 g/4.2 oz) green bell pepper, sliced
- 1 medium (120 g/4.2 oz) red bell pepper, sliced
- 2 large (128 g/4.5 oz) celery stalks, sliced
- 2 cups (226 g/8 oz) shredded Cheddar cheese, divided
- 2 medium (30 g/1.1 oz) spring onions, sliced

Instructions

Mix the ranch seasoning with the sour cream and set aside. Bring a saucepan filled with salted water to a boil. Add the cauliflower and broccoli. Cook for 4 to 5 minutes, until crisp-tender. Drain and set aside.

Preheat the oven to 375°F (190°C, or gas mark 5). Heat a large skillet or casserole dish greased with the ghee. Once hot, add the chicken and cook over medium-high heat for 5 to 7 minutes, until browned on all sides. Add the green pepper, red pepper, and celery. Cook for 1 to 2 minutes, stirring frequently. Add the steamed broccoli and cauliflower.

Take off the heat, and add the seasoned sour cream and Cheddar cheese (reserve some cheese for topping). Mix using a spatula until all the ingredients are combined. Top with the reserved cheese and transfer to the oven. Bake for 15 to 20 minutes, or until the top is golden brown and crisped up. When done, remove from the oven and set aside to cool. Top with the spring onions. To store, let it cool, and refrigerate in an airtight container for up to 4 days or freeze for up to 3 months.

NUTRITION FACTS PER SERVING:
Total carbs: 12.2 g / Fiber: 4 g / Net carbs: 8.2 g / Protein: 32.9 g / Fat: 29.7 g / Energy: 443 kcal
Macronutrient ratio: Calories from carbs (8%), protein (30%), fat (62%)

Chicken Tikka Masala

There's nothing as comforting as tender chicken cooked in creamy coconut milk and a homemade curry paste, so put down that take-out menu and get ready to make the best—and easiest!—keto-friendly chicken tikka masala you've ever tasted.

Ingredients

- ¼ cup (55 g/1.9 oz) ghee or other healthy cooking fat (see page 14)
- 1 small (70 g/2.5 oz) yellow onion, chopped
- 1 recipe Tikka Masala Curry Paste (page 23)
- 1 large (240 g/8.5 oz) tomato, diced (or use canned diced tomatoes)
- 1½ cup (360 ml) chicken stock (page 28)
- 2.7 pounds (1.2 kg) boneless and skinless chicken thighs, cut into 1½-inch (4-cm) chunks
- 1½ cans (600 ml/20 fl oz) coconut milk
- Salt and pepper
- Suggested sides: cauli-rice (page 18) or shirataki rice (page 19)
- Optional: ⅓ cup (30 g/1.1 oz) flaked toasted almonds and fresh cilantro for garnish

Instructions

Preheat the slow cooker. Grease a large heavy-based saucepan or Dutch oven with the ghee. Add the onion and cook over medium-high heat for 5 to 8 minutes, or until lightly browned. Add the tikka masala paste and cook for a minute, stirring frequently. Mix in the tomatoes and stock, and transfer the mixture to the slow cooker. Add the chicken chunks, cover with a lid, and cook on low for 4 to 6 hours. Stir in the coconut milk in the last 30 minutes of the cooking process.

When done, taste and season if needed. Serve with steamed cauli-rice or shirataki rice. Optionally, top with flaked toasted almonds and fresh cilantro. To store, let it cool, and refrigerate for up to 4 days or freeze for up to 3 months.

NUTRITION FACTS PER SERVING:
Total carbs: 8.5 g / Fiber: 2.6 g / Net carbs: 5.9 g / Protein: 32.7 g / Fat: 34.7 g / Energy: 468 kcal
Macronutrient ratio: Calories from carbs (5%), protein (28%), fat (67%)

Chicken Paprikash

MAKES: 8 servings
PREPARATION TIME: 20 minutes
COOKING TIME: 6 hours

Like my Hungarian Goulash (page 74), this paprika-spiked Hungarian dish is really easy to prepare, and it's a major crowd-pleaser, too. Make a batch next time unexpected guests turn up, and ladle it over cauli-rice (page 18) or shirataki rice (page 19).

Ingredients

- 8 large (1.6 kg/3.5 lb) bone-in chicken thighs, trimmed of excess fat and skin (or 1.2 kg/2.7 lb boneless chicken)
- Salt and pepper
- 2 tablespoons (30 g/1.1 oz) ghee or other healthy cooking fat (see page 14), divided
- 1 medium (110 g/3.9 oz) yellow onion, chopped
- 2 cloves garlic, minced
- 1 medium (120 g/4.2 oz) red bell pepper, sliced
- 1 medium (120 g/4.2 oz) green bell pepper, sliced
- 1 cup (240 ml) chicken stock (page 28), divided
- 1 teaspoon dried marjoram
- ¼ cup (28 g/1 oz) paprika, divided
- 1 cup (240 g/8.5 oz) canned chopped tomatoes
- 4 egg yolks
- 1 cup (230 g/8.1 oz) full-fat sour cream
- Fresh parsley for garnish
- Suggested sides: cauli-rice (page 18) or shirataki rice (page 19)

Instructions

Preheat the slow cooker. Season the chicken thighs with salt on all sides. Heat a large skillet or casserole dish greased with 1 tablespoon (15 g) of the ghee. Once hot, add the chicken thighs in a single layer, skin-side down. Cook over medium-high heat for 5 minutes. Turn on the other side and cook for another 3 minutes. Remove the chicken from the pan and set aside on a plate.

Grease the pan with the remaining 1 tablespoon (15 g) ghee. Add the onion and cook over medium-high heat for 5 to 8 minutes, or until lightly browned. Add the garlic and peppers. Cook for a minute and add ½ cup (120 ml) of the chicken stock, marjoram, black pepper to taste, and 1 tablespoon (7 g) of the paprika. Add the tomatoes and heat through.

Transfer the mixture to a slow cooker and add back the browned chicken thighs. Cook on low for 5 hours. After 5 hours, use tongs to gently remove the chicken thighs and set aside on a plate. Beat the egg yolks with the remaining ½ cup (120 ml) chicken stock. Slowly drizzle into the slow cooker while stirring. Add the remaining 3 tablespoons (21 g) paprika and sour cream, and combine well. Add back the chicken, cover with a lid, and cook for another hour. When done, garnish with fresh parsley, taste, and season if needed. Serve with steamed cauli-rice or shirataki rice.

TIP: Are you dairy-free? Instead of 1 cup (230 g/8.1 oz) full-fat sour cream, try ¾ cup (180 g/6.4 oz) coconut cream with 2 tablespoons (30 ml) lemon juice or apple cider vinegar.

NUTRITION FACTS PER SERVING (WITHOUT SIDE DISH):
Total carbs: 7.2 g / Fiber: 2.3 g / Net carbs: 4.9 g / Protein: 24.8 g / Fat: 56 g / Energy: 632 kcal
Macronutrient ratio: Calories from carbs (3%), protein (16%), fat (81%)

Whole Slow Cooker Chicken

Believe it or not, it's super-easy to roast a whole chicken in a slow cooker. The skin won't get crispy, as with oven roasting, but the meat becomes amazingly tender and juicy. For best results, lather the chicken in fragrant herb-and-spice rubs before cooking.

Ingredients

CHICKEN:

1 whole chicken (about
    1.4 kg/3 lb, bones included),
    will yield about 50% meat
1 tablespoon (15 g/0.5 oz) ghee
    or other healthy cooking fat
    (see page 14), divided
1 small (70 g/2.5 oz) yellow
    onion, chopped
2 cloves garlic, minced

CURRIED RUB:

2 tablespoons (30 g/1.1 oz) ghee
    or other healthy cooking fat
    (see page 14), softened
2 teaspoons curry powder
1 teaspoon fine sea salt, or to
    taste
½ teaspoon onion powder
½ teaspoon garlic powder
½ teaspoon ground black pepper
½ teaspoon paprika
¼ teaspoon ground ginger
¼ teaspoon ground caraway

Instructions

Preheat the slow cooker. Rinse the chicken under cold water, then pat dry inside and out using a paper towel. Place on a chopping board.

In a bowl, combine all the ingredients for the rub and set aside.

Grease a large heavy-based saucepan or Dutch oven with the ghee. Add the onion and cook over medium-high heat for 5 to 8 minutes, until lightly browned. Add the garlic, cook for 1 minute, and transfer to the slow cooker.

Use your hands to create a pocket between the breasts, thighs, and drumsticks and the chicken skin. Push half of the flavored rub under the skin and rub the remaining mixture all over the chicken. Tuck the wing tips under the chicken and tie the legs together using kitchen string.

Grease the saucepan where you cooked the onion with the remaining tablespoon (15 g) of ghee and cook the chicken until browned all over. Transfer to the slow cooker on top of the browned onion and garlic. Cook on low for 6 hours. Serve with low-carb veggies or Make-Ahead Slow Cooker Mash (page 48). To store, let it cool, and refrigerate for up to 3 days.

NUTRITION FACTS PER SERVING (¼ CHICKEN):
Total carbs: 3.5 g / Fiber: 1 g / Net carbs: 2.5 g / Protein: 33.1 g / Fat: 42.5 g / Energy: 529 kcal
Macronutrient ratio: Calories from carbs (2%), protein (25%), fat (73%)

TIPS FOR MORE RUBS

- If using any spicy rub, make sure you use disposable gloves!

- PESTO RUB: Use ¼ cup (60 g/2.1 oz) Red Pesto (page 37). For an extra flavor boost, add 1 quartered lemon and a few thyme sprigs inside the chicken cavity, and then tie the legs with kitchen string.

- THAI RUB: Mix 2 tablespoons (30 g/1.1 oz) Thai Curry Paste (page 40) with 2 tablespoons (30 g/1.1 oz) softened cooking fat of choice.

- MOROCCAN RUB: Mix 2 tablespoons (30 g/1.1 oz) Harissa Paste (page 39) with 2 tablespoons (30 g/1.1 oz) softened cooking fat of choice.

Moroccan Chicken Stew

Since it's naturally low-carb, harissa paste is a great way to add spicy, smoky flavor to almost any dish—like this stew, which is a close cousin of traditional Moroccan tagine. When you make it in a slow cooker, you'll end up with perfectly tender, flavorful chicken every single time.

Ingredients

2.7 pounds (1.2 kg) boneless and skinless chicken thighs, cut into 1½-inch (4-cm) chunks

½ cup (120 g/4.2 oz) mild Harissa Paste (page 39)

2 tablespoons (30 g/1.1 oz) ghee or other healthy cooking fat (see page 14)

1 small (70 g/2.5 oz) yellow onion, chopped

½ teaspoon ground cinnamon

½ teaspoon ground ginger

½ teaspoon ground cumin

½ teaspoon black pepper

1 teaspoon fine sea salt, or to taste

1½ cups (320 ml) chicken stock (page 28) or bone broth (page 44)

1 cup (240 g/8.5 oz) canned chopped tomatoes

3 tablespoons (45 ml) fresh lemon juice

½ cup (50 g/1.8 oz) pitted green olives, sliced

1 medium (250 g/8.8 oz) eggplant, cut into 1-inch (2.5-cm) pieces

2 cups (235 g/8.3 oz) diced pumpkin, cut into 1-inch (2.5-cm) pieces

Suggested sides: cauli-rice (page 18) or shirataki rice (page 19)
Optional toppings: ½ cup (45 g/1.6 oz) toasted flaked almonds, 1 cup (230 g/8.1 oz) full-fat sour cream, and fresh cilantro

Instructions

Place the chicken chunks in a bowl and cover in the harissa paste. Cover and let it marinate for 30 minutes, or up to 2 hours in the fridge.

Preheat the slow cooker. Grease a large heavy-based saucepan or Dutch oven with the ghee. Add the onion and cook over medium-high heat for 5 to 8 minutes, until lightly browned. Add the marinated chicken, cinnamon, ginger, cumin, black pepper, and salt. Cook for 2 to 3 minutes, stirring frequently. Add the chicken stock and heat through. Transfer to the slow cooker and add the tomatoes, lemon juice, olives, eggplant, and pumpkin.

Cover with a lid, and cook on low for 6 hours or on high for 3 hours. When done, taste and season if needed. Serve with steamed cauli-rice or shirataki rice. Optionally, top with toasted flaked almonds, sour cream, and cilantro. To store, let it cool, and refrigerate for up to 4 days or freeze for up to 3 months.

NUTRITION FACTS PER SERVING:
Total carbs: 9.6 g / Fiber: 3.1 g / Net carbs: 6.5 g / Protein: 23.7 g / Fat: 50.9 g / Energy: 589 kcal
Macronutrient ratio: Calories from carbs (4%), protein (16%), fat (80%)

MAKES: 4 servings (20 meatballs)
PREPARATION TIME: 15 minutes
COOKING TIME: 3 to 4 hours

Festive Turkey Meatballs

We all know that homemade cranberry sauce goes best with roast turkey, especially during the festive season. Here, though, I've transformed that classic pairing into tender, juicy turkey meatballs drenched in a tangy cranberry "gravy." Your guests will be seriously impressed!

Ingredients

MEATBALLS:

¼ cup (55 g/1.9 oz) ghee or other healthy cooking fat (see page 14), divided

1 small (70 g/2.5 oz) yellow onion, chopped

2 cloves garlic, minced

1.1 pounds (500 g) ground turkey

1 large egg

2 tablespoons (16 g/0.6 oz) coconut flour or ½ cup (50 g/1.8 oz) almond flour

½ teaspoon dried thyme

2 tablespoons (8 g/0.3 oz) freshly chopped parsley, plus more for garnish

½ teaspoon fine sea salt, or to taste

¼ teaspoon ground black pepper

SAUCE:

½ cup (125 g/4.4 oz) Cranberry Sauce (page 43)

½ cup (120 ml) chicken stock (page 28)

Suggested side dish: Make-Ahead Slow Cooker Mash (page 48)

Instructions

Preheat the slow cooker. Grease a large skillet with 2 tablespoons (30 g) of the ghee. Add the onion and cook over medium-high heat for 5 to 8 minutes, until lightly browned. Add the garlic, cook for another minute, and set aside.

Place the turkey, egg, coconut flour, thyme, fresh parsley, salt, pepper, and cooked onions with garlic in a bowl. Mix until well combined. Using your hands, create 20 meatballs (about 32 g/1.1 oz each).

To brown the meatballs, grease a large pan with the remaining 2 tablespoons (30 g) ghee and place over medium heat. When hot, add the meatballs in a single layer. Cook for 2 minutes on each side, turning with a fork until browned on all sides and cooked through. Transfer the meatballs to the slow cooker.

Add the cranberry sauce and chicken stock to the skillet where you cooked the meatballs and bring to a boil. Cook for a minute, and pour into the slow cooker over the meatballs. Cook on low for 3 to 4 hours. Serve with Make-Ahead Slow Cooker Mash (page 48) or low-carb veggies. To store, let it cool, and refrigerate for up to 4 days.

TIP: Just like the Make-Ahead Freezer Meatballs (page 45), these turkey meatballs can be prepared ahead of time and frozen for up to 3 months.

NUTRITION FACTS PER SERVING (5 MEATBALLS):
Total carbs: 6.7 g / Fiber: 2.2 g / Net carbs: 4.5 g / Protein: 24.4 g / Fat: 31.9 g / Energy: 413 kcal
Macronutrient ratio: Calories from carbs (5%), protein (24%), fat (71%)

MAKES: 6 servings
PREPARATION TIME: 20 minutes
COOKING TIME: 4 to 5 hours

Beef Bourguignon

This classic French dish might sound intimidating, but it's actually incredibly easy to make. Dry red wine lends an earthy, rich flavor to the slow-cooked meat, which is wonderful with roasted green beans or steamed leafy greens. (Only add the carrot if it fits within your daily carbohydrate limit.)

Ingredients

BOUQUET GARNI:

2 sprigs fresh parsley and thyme

1 teaspoon peppercorns

3 whole cloves

3 bay leaves

STEW:

2 pounds (900 g) beef chuck steak or brisket

Salt

3 tablespoons (45 g/1.6 oz) ghee or other healthy cooking fat (see page 14), divided

1 medium (110 g/3.9 oz) white onion, chopped

3 cloves garlic, crushed

Optional: 1 medium (60 g/2.1 oz) carrot, sliced

1 bottle (750 ml) dry red wine such as Burgundy (see page 31 for substitutions)

1 tablespoon (15 g/0.5 oz) unsweetened tomato paste

8 slices (240 g/8.5 oz) bacon

4 cups (300 g/10.6 oz) sliced white mushrooms

1 teaspoon fine sea salt, or to taste

Suggested side: Make-Ahead Slow Cooker Mash (page 48) or roasted green beans

Instructions

Preheat the slow cooker. Make the bouquet garni by placing all the herbs in a piece of cheesecloth and tying with unwaxed kitchen string.

Cut the beef into large chunks and season with some salt. Heat a Dutch oven or a heavy-based pot greased with 2 tablespoons (30 g/1.1 oz) of the ghee. Fry the beef chunks in batches over medium-high heat until golden brown on all sides, about 5 minutes. Remove the chunks from the pot and place them in the slow cooker.

Add the onion, crushed garlic, and carrot (if using) to the pot where you browned the beef and lower the heat. Pour in the red wine and add the tomato paste. Bring to a boil and mix well with a spatula, scraping the caramelized cooking juices from the bottom of the pot. Pour into the slow cooker. Add the bouquet garni, cover with a lid, and cook on high for 4 to 5 hours. Remove the bouquet garni when the meat is cooked.

Grease a pan with the remaining 1 tablespoon (15 g) ghee and crisp up the bacon over medium heat for about 5 minutes. Add the mushrooms and cook for another 4 to 5 minutes, or until tender and browned. Take off the heat and place in the slow cooker with the beef. Mix until well combined. Serve with Make-Ahead Slow Cooker Mash (page 48) or roasted green beans. To store, let it cool, and refrigerate for up to 4 days or freeze for up to 3 months.

NUTRITION FACTS PER SERVING:
Total carbs: 8.3 g / Fiber: 1.4 g / Net carbs: 6.9 g / Protein: 36.7 g / Fat: 45 g / Energy: 678 kcal
Macronutrient ratio: Calories from carbs (5%), protein (25%), fat (70%)

MAKES: 6 servings
PREPARATION TIME: 15 minutes
+ freezing
COOKING TIME: 30 minutes

Beef Fricassee Casserole

Featuring beef in place of the customary chicken, this casserole is an inventive twist on a classic French fricassee. In it, beef and low-carb vegetables are mingled in a creamy sauce before being crowned with cheese and broiled until bubbling. Heavenly!

Ingredients

- 1.3 pounds (600 g) beef sirloin (rump) steak
- Salt and pepper
- ¼ cup (55 g/1.9 oz) ghee or other healthy cooking fat (see page 14), divided
- 1 small (70 g/2.5 oz) yellow onion, chopped
- 2 cloves garlic, minced
- 2 bay leaves, crumbled
- 2 large (128 g/4.5 oz) celery stalks, sliced
- 1 medium (85 g/3 oz) leek, sliced
- 4 cups (280 g/9.9 oz) sliced white mushrooms
- 1 medium (400 g/14.1 oz) broccoli or broccolini, roughly chopped
- 1 cup (240 ml) bone broth (page 44) or chicken stock (page 28)
- ½ cup (115 g/4 oz) full-fat sour cream
- 1 teaspoon paprika
- ⅛ teaspoon cayenne pepper
- 1½ cups (180 g/6.3 oz) grated Swiss or Cheddar cheese
- 2 tablespoons (8 g/0.3 oz) freshly chopped herbs such as parsley, oregano, and thyme

Instructions

Slice the steak into thin strips (for easy slicing, freeze the steak for 30 to 60 minutes). Season with salt and pepper. Heat a casserole dish greased with half of the ghee. Add the beef slices and quickly fry them in batches on both sides until browned. Remove from the dish and set aside for later.

Grease the pan with the remaining ghee and add the onion. Cook over medium-high heat for 5 to 8 minutes, until lightly browned. Add the garlic, crumbled bay leaves, celery, and leek, and cook for 2 minutes. Add the mushrooms, broccoli, broth, sour cream, paprika, and cayenne pepper. Cover with a lid and cook over medium-low heat for 5 to 6 minutes, until the broccoli is tender.

Take off the heat. Add back the cooked steak, mix, and sprinkle with the Swiss cheese. Place under a broiler and cook on high until the cheese is melted, about 5 minutes. When done, remove from the oven, set aside to cool and then garnish with the fresh herbs. To store, let it cool, and refrigerate for up to 4 days or freeze for up to 3 months.

NUTRITION FACTS PER SERVING:
Total carbs: 11 g / Fiber: 3.2 g / Net carbs: 7.8 g / Protein: 34.7 g / Fat: 34.7 g / Energy: 492 kcal
Macronutrient ratio: Calories from carbs (6%), protein (29%), fat (65%)

Caribbean Beef Stew

There's nothing boring about this hearty Jamaican-style beef stew. Garlic, ginger, chile, and allspice put a spring in its step, and it's full of low-carb vegetables, too. Try it over Cauli-Rice, or with a mess of leafy greens.

Ingredients

2 pounds (900 g) beef chuck steak

¾ teaspoon fine sea salt, or to taste

Ground black pepper

2 tablespoons (30 g/1.1 oz) ghee or other healthy cooking fat (see page 14), divided

1 small (70 g/2.5 oz) yellow onion, chopped

2 cloves garlic, minced

1-inch piece (6 g/0.2 oz) ginger, finely chopped

1 small (14 g/0.5 oz) red chile pepper, chopped

2 cups (480 ml) bone broth (page 44) or water

1 cup (240 g/8.5 oz) canned diced tomatoes

2 tablespoons (30 ml) coconut aminos

1 tablespoon (7 g/0.2 oz) paprika

2 bay leaves

¼ teaspoon allspice

1 medium (120 g/4.2 oz) red bell pepper, sliced

1½ cups (174 g/6.1 oz) diced pumpkin

1 medium (200 g/7.1 oz) zucchini, diced

2 tablespoons (8 g/0.3 oz) freshly chopped cilantro, parsley, or spring onion for garnish

Suggested side: cauli-rice (page 18) or shirataki rice (page 19)

Instructions

Preheat the slow cooker. Cut the beef into large (about 1½-inch/4-cm) chunks, and season with salt and pepper. To brown the beef, grease a large heavy-based saucepan or Dutch oven with half of the ghee. Cook the beef in batches until browned on all sides and transfer to the slow cooker.

Grease the saucepan with the remaining ghee. Add the onion and cook over medium-high heat for 5 to 8 minutes, until lightly browned. Add the garlic, ginger, and chile pepper, and cook for 1 to 2 minutes. Pour in the bone broth to deglaze the saucepan, scraping the browned bits off the bottom. Pour into the slow cooker over the browned beef. Add the tomatoes, coconut aminos, paprika, bay leaves, and allspice. Combine with a spatula, cover with a lid, and cook on high for 4 hours.

After 2 hours of cooking, mix in the red pepper, pumpkin, and zucchini. Cover with a lid and cook for another 2 hours. Garnish with fresh herbs, and serve with cauli-rice (page 18). To store, let it cool, and refrigerate for up to 4 days or freeze for up to 3 months.

NUTRITION FACTS PER SERVING:
Total carbs: 8.6 g / Fiber: 2 g / Net carbs: 6.6 g / Protein: 31.7 g / Fat: 33.4 g / Energy: 464 kcal
Macronutrient ratio: Calories from carbs (6%), protein (28%), fat (66%)

Osso Buco with Gremolata

MAKES: 8 servings
PREPARATION TIME: 20 minutes
COOKING TIME: 4 to 5 hours

Osso buco, which translates as "pierced bone" in Italian, involves cooking veal shanks on low for several hours, and they're well worth the wait: they're amazingly tender and juicy, thanks, in part, to the luscious bone marrow. Serve with a spoonful of garlicky, lemony gremolata.

Ingredients

BOUQUET GARNI:

3 sprigs fresh thyme
1 sprig fresh rosemary
2 bay leaves
2 cloves
1 teaspoon whole black peppercorns

STEW:

4 whole bone-in veal shanks (1.8 kg/4 lb), will yield about 60% meat
Salt and pepper
3 tablespoons (45 g/1.6 oz) ghee or other healthy cooking fat (see page 14), divided
1 small (70 g/2.5 oz) yellow onion, sliced
2 cloves garlic, minced
3 large (192 g/6.8 oz) celery stalks, sliced
1 cup (240 ml) bone broth (page 44) or water
1 cup (240 g/8.5 oz) canned or fresh diced tomatoes
2 tablespoons (30 g/1.1 oz) unsweetened tomato paste
1 cup (240 ml) dry white wine (see page 31 for substitutions)

Suggested sides: cauli-rice (page 18), Make-Ahead Slow Cooker Mash (page 48) or other low-carb vegetable sides (see page 21)

GREMOLATA:

½ cup (30 g/1.1 oz) chopped parsley
2 cloves garlic, crushed
Zest from 1 lemon

Instructions

Preheat the slow cooker. Make the bouquet garni by placing all the herbs in a piece of cheesecloth and tying with unwaxed kitchen string.

Pat dry the veal shanks using a paper towel. Secure the shanks to the bone with kitchen string, and season with salt and pepper.

Grease a large heavy-based saucepan or Dutch oven with half of the ghee. Brown the veal shanks on all sides over high heat. Remove the shanks and set aside.

Grease the saucepan with the remaining ghee. Add the onion and cook over medium-high heat for 5 to 8 minutes, or until lightly browned. Add the garlic, celery, bone broth, tomatoes, tomato paste, and white wine. Transfer to the slow cooker and add the prepared bouquet garni. Add the browned veal shanks in a single layer, and cover with a lid. Cook on high for 4 hours or on low for 8 hours. When done, remove and discard the bouquet garni and kitchen string. Serve with cauli-rice or other low-carb veggies. To store, refrigerate for up to 4 days, or shred the meat off the bones and freeze for up to 3 months.

NUTRITION FACTS PER SERVING:
Total carbs: 4.5 g / Fiber: 1.1 g / Net carbs: 3.4 g / Protein: 24.5 g / Fat: 23 g / Energy: 350 kcal
Macronutrient ratio: Calories from carbs (4%), protein (31%), fat (65%)

Stuffed Cabbage Rolls with Spicy Hollandaise

Once they've been blanched, vitamin-C-rich cabbage leaves are handy vehicles for all sorts of fillings, like these fun-to-eat low-carb cabbage rolls, which are packed with beef, Cauli-Rice, and spices.

Ingredients

CABBAGE ROLLS:

1.1 pounds (500 g) minced beef

2 cups (240 g/8.5 oz) uncooked cauli-rice (page 18)

1 small (70 g/2.5 oz) yellow onion, chopped

2 cloves garlic, minced

1 large egg

½ teaspoon fine sea salt

¼ teaspoon ground black pepper

1 teaspoon Dijon mustard

2 tablespoons (8 g/0.3 oz) freshly chopped parsley

1 teaspoon paprika

1 medium or 2 small (500 g/ 1.1 lb) savoy cabbage

1 cup (240 ml) bone broth (page 44)

Instructions

Preheat the slow cooker. In a bowl, combine the the beef, cauli-rice, onion, garlic, egg, salt, pepper, Dijon mustard, parsley, and paprika.

Separate the outer 12 cabbage leaves and place them in a pot of boiling salted water. Blanch until limp, 1 to 2 minutes. Transfer the leaves to a large bowl filled with ice water. Drain and pat dry. Remove the core of the cabbage, slice the remaining leaves, place them in the slow cooker, and add the bone broth.

Place the cabbage leaves on a chopping board. Using a paring knife, shave down the thick cabbage stems in the middle. Do not cut through the cabbage leaves. Place some of the meat filling (about 70 g/2.5 oz per leaf) in the middle of the cabbage. (The exact amount depends on the size of the leaf. Do not overfill the leaves.) Roll the cabbage leaf up, folding both sides over the filling, creating a small parcel. Place the cabbage parcels seam-side down in the slow cooker in two or three layers, and cook on low for 6 hours.

To make the hollandaise sauce, gently melt the butter and set aside. Fill a medium saucepan with 1 cup (240 ml) water and bring to a boil. In a separate bowl, mix the egg yolks with the lemon juice, water, and Dijon mustard. (Use the leftover egg whites to make Sourdough Keto Buns on page 52). Place the bowl over the saucepan filled with water. (The water should not touch the bottom of the bowl.) Keep mixing until

NUTRITION FACTS PER SERVING (3 CABBAGE ROLLS WITH 3 TABLESPOONS [40 G/1.4 OZ] OF HOLLANDAISE):
Total carbs: 14.1 g / Fiber: 5.7 g / Net carbs: 8.4 g / Protein: 30.3 g / Fat: 49.4 g / Energy: 613 kcal
Macronutrient ratio: Calories from carbs (6%), protein (20%), fat (74%)

SPICY HOLLANDAISE:

6 tablespoons (85 g/3 oz) butter, ghee, or bacon grease

3 egg yolks

3 tablespoons (45 ml) lemon juice

2 to 3 tablespoons (30 to 45 ml) water

¾ teaspoon Dijon mustard

1 tablespoon (15 g/0.5 oz) sriracha sauce or tomato paste for non-spicy

the sauce starts to thicken. Slowly pour the melted butter into the mixture until thick and creamy, and stir constantly. If the sauce is too thick, add a splash of water. Mix in the sriracha sauce and set aside. Cover with a lid and keep warm for up to 2 hours. Serve with the cooked stuffed cabbage leaves. Do not reheat the hollandaise or it will separate. Always make a fresh batch. To store the cabbage rolls, let them cool, and refrigerate for up to 4 days or freeze for up to 3 months.

Autumn Beef & Vegetable Stew

When the weather turns colder, we reach for woolly sweaters, autumn spices, and plenty of comfort food, like this beef stew. It's an all-time slow-cooker favorite in my house, and it's perfectly balanced for a keto diet: it's high in fat, low in carbs, and rich in electrolytes.

Ingredients

3.3 pounds (1.5 kg) beef chuck or shin steaks

1½ teaspoon fine sea salt, or to taste

Ground black pepper

½ cup (110 g/3.9 oz) ghee or other healthy cooking fat (see page 14), divided

1 medium (110 g/3.9 oz) white onion, chopped

4 cloves garlic, minced

1 can (400 g/14.1 oz) chopped tomatoes, unsweetened

1 cup (240 ml) bone broth (page 44), vegetable stock (page 28), or water

2 tablespoons ground cumin

1 tablespoon paprika

1 teaspoon ground ginger

1 teaspoon chili powder

1 teaspoon ground coriander

1 teaspoon turmeric powder

2 cinnamon sticks

2 bay leaves

1 large (600 g/1.3 lb) rutabaga, peeled and cut into 1-inch (2.5-cm) pieces

4 or 5 medium (1 kg/2.2 lb) zucchini or marrow squash, diced

Fresh parsley or cilantro

Instructions

Preheat a 5- to 6-quart (4.7- to 5.7-L) slow cooker. Using a paper towel, pat dry the beef, and season with salt and pepper on both sides. Place 2 or 3 steaks at a time in a hot pan greased with half of the ghee and sear until lightly browned all over. When done, transfer to the preheated slow cooker.

Grease the saucepan with the remaining ghee. Add the onion and cook over medium-high heat for 5 to 8 minutes, or until lightly browned. Add the garlic, tomatoes, broth, cumin, paprika, ginger, chili powder, coriander, and turmeric. Bring to a boil, and then pour into the slow cooker over the meat. Add the cinnamon sticks and bay leaves. Cover with a lid and cook on high for 5 to 5½ hours.

After the meat has been cooking for 3 hours, use a spatula to push the meat to one side of the slow cooker and add the rutabaga and zucchini next to it. Cover and cook in the juices for another 2 to 2½ hours. The stew is cooked when the rutabaga and zucchini are fork-tender. Discard the bay leaves and cinnamon sticks. Season with more salt and pepper, and serve with fresh herbs. To store, let it cool, and refrigerate for up to 4 days or freeze for up to 3 months.

NUTRITION FACTS PER SERVING:
Total carbs: 12.7 g / Fiber: 3.6 g / Net carbs: 9.1 g / Protein: 31.9 g / Fat: 39.5 g / Energy: 534 kcal
Macronutrient ratio: Calories from carbs (7%), protein (25%), fat (68%)

Beef Short Ribs with Coleslaw

What's the best way to make perfectly tender beef ribs? Pop them into a slow cooker, of course: afterward, it takes just a few minutes to finish them off in the oven. And for a complete meal, you'll want to serve them alongside crisp, creamy, tangy coleslaw.

Ingredients

SPICE RUB:

1 tablespoon (10 g/0.3 oz) garlic powder
1 tablespoon (7 g/0.2 oz) onion powder
2 teaspoons (5 g/0.2 oz) paprika
2 teaspoons fine sea salt
1 tablespoon (5 g/0.2 oz) oregano
¼ teaspoon cayenne pepper

SHORT RIBS:

4 pounds (1.8 kg) beef short ribs, will yield about 50% meat
½ cup (120 g/4.2 oz) Sweet & Sour BBQ Sauce (page 42), plus optionally more to serve with

COLESLAW:

1.3 pounds (600 g) sliced green or white cabbage, core removed
1 small (60 g/2.1 oz) red onion, sliced
½ cup (110 g/3.9 oz) mayonnaise (page 25)
3 tablespoons (45 ml) fresh lemon juice
¼ cup (15 g/0.5 oz) chopped parsley or chives
½ teaspoon celery seeds
Salt and pepper

Instructions

Preheat the slow cooker and pour in ¼ cup (60 ml) of water. Prepare the rub by mixing all the spices and set aside.

Pat dry the ribs using a paper towel and cover the short ribs in the spice rub, pressing it all over the ribs. Optionally, cover and marinate in the fridge for up to 8 hours. Transfer the ribs to the slow cooker and cook on high for 4 to 5 hours, until the meat is tender.

Prepare the coleslaw. Using your food processor's slicing blade, thinly slice the cabbage, and then place in a large mixing bowl. Add the red onion, mayonnaise, lemon juice, parsley, and celery seeds. Season with salt and pepper to taste, and mix well.

After 4 to 5 hours of cooking the ribs, using tongs, remove the ribs from the slow cooker and place on a baking sheet lined with heavy-duty parchment paper. Preheat the broiler. Brush the ribs with the BBQ sauce on all sides and place the ribs under the broiler. Cook on high for 8 to 10 minutes, turning halfway through. Serve with the prepared coleslaw. To store both the ribs and the coleslaw, refrigerate for up to 4 days. To freeze the ribs, shred off the bones and freeze for up to 3 months (meat only).

NUTRITION FACTS PER SERVING:
Total carbs: 11.7 g / Fiber: 4.1 g / Net carbs: 7.6 g / Protein: 28.5 g / Fat: 44.4 g / Energy: 547 kcal
Macronutrient ratio: Calories from carbs (6%), protein (21%), fat (73%)

Slow Cooker Beef Fajitas

Made with low-carb Keto Tortillas (page 46), these beef fajitas are the real deal. Create a dinnertime "fajita bar" by offering toppings—like sour cream, diced avocado, tomatoes, green pepper, grated Cheddar or Manchego cheese, lime wedges, and cilantro—separately, and let everyone build their own. That's half the fun!

Ingredients

2.65 pounds (1.2 kg) beef chuck steak
1 teaspoon salt, or to taste
Ground black pepper
2 tablespoons (30 g/1.1 oz) ghee or other healthy cooking fat (see page 14), divided
1 small (70 g/2.5 oz) yellow onion, sliced
3 cloves garlic, minced
14.1 ounces (400 g) canned chopped tomatoes
2 tablespoons (30 g/1.1 oz) unsweetened tomato paste
2 teaspoons ground cumin
2 teaspoons ground coriander
1 teaspoon smoked paprika
1 teaspoon chili powder
8 Keto Tortillas of choice, soft or crisped up into taco shells (see page 47)
Suggested sides: sour cream, diced avocado, tomatoes, green pepper, grated Cheddar or Manchego cheese, lime wedges, and cilantro

Instructions

Preheat the slow cooker. Cut the beef into large (about 1½-inch/4-cm) chunks and season with salt and pepper. To brown the beef, grease a large heavy-based saucepan or Dutch oven with half of the ghee. Cook the beef in batches until browned on all sides and transfer to the slow cooker.

Grease the saucepan with the remaining ghee. Add the onion and cook over medium-high heat for 5 to 8 minutes, until lightly browned. Add the garlic and cook for a minute. Add the tomatoes and bring to a boil, scraping the browned bits from the bottom of the pan. Pour into the slow cooker over the browned beef. Add the tomato paste, cumin, coriander, paprika, and chili powder. Cover with a lid. Cook on high for 3 to 4 hours or on low for 6 to 8 hours.

When done, shred the beef with a fork. Serve with the tortillas and sides of choice. To store, refrigerate the meat for up to 5 days or freeze for up to 3 months.

NUTRITION FACTS PER SERVING (MEAT + CURRIED TORTILLA):
Total carbs: 12 g / Fiber: 7.1 g / Net carbs: 4.9 g / Protein: 34.8 g / Fat: 41.3 g / Energy: 554 kcal
Macronutrient ratio: Calories from carbs (4%), protein (26%), fat (70%)

Quick Meatball Casserole

Here's what to do if you're craving an old-fashioned meatball sub: Make this low-fuss casserole tonight and serve it with Sourdough Keto Buns (page 52). What makes it so simple? It calls for Make-Ahead Freezer Meatballs, which keep prep to a minimum, plus just a few other basic ingredients.

Ingredients

1 recipe marinara sauce (page 25), skip the olive oil

½ cup (120 ml) bone broth (page 44) or chicken stock (page 28)

½ recipe Make-Ahead Freezer Meatballs (page 45), 32 meatballs

1½ cups (170 g/6 oz) shredded mozzarella cheese

1 cup (90 g/3.2 oz) grated Parmesan cheese

Salt and pepper

Fresh basil for garnish

Suggested sides: Sourdough Keto Buns (page 52) or zoodles (page 18)

Instructions

Prepare the marinara sauce. (Make it without the olive oil, as there's plenty of healthy fats and you don't want to make the finished dish too greasy.)

Heat a large skillet or a casserole dish over medium heat. Add the marinara sauce, broth, and meatballs. Bring to a boil, cover with a lid, and cook on low for 10 to 12 minutes (if using fresh meatballs) or up to 20 minutes (if using frozen meatballs). Remove the lid and cook for another 5 minutes, until the sauce thickens slightly.

Sprinkle with both mozzarella and Parmesan, and place under a broiler. Cook on high until the cheese is melted, about 5 minutes. Season with salt and pepper to taste, and garnish with fresh basil. Serve with buns or zoodles. To store, let the meatballs cool, and refrigerate for up to 4 days or freeze for up to 3 months.

NUTRITION FACTS PER SERVING (4 MEATBALLS):
Total carbs: 4.3 g / Fiber: 0.7 g / Net carbs: 3.6 g / Protein: 31.8 g / Fat: 32.5 g / Energy: 443 kcal
Macronutrient ratio: Calories from carbs (3%), protein (29%), fat (68%)

Three Meat & Liver Stew

If you've never tried oxtail or marrowbones before, start here. Both of them add deep flavor and texture to a dish, especially when they're paired with leaner cuts of meat. And lamb's liver adds a whack of valuable nutrients, like protein, iron, and vitamin A.

Ingredients

STEW:

2 pounds (900 g) oxtail, will yield about 50% meat

Salt and pepper

2 tablespoons (30 g/1.1 oz) ghee or other healthy cooking fat (see page 14), divided

2 or 3 pieces marrowbones

1 whole chicken breast, bone in and skin on (400 g/14.1 oz)

12 ounces (340 g) lamb liver, sliced

1 medium (110 g/3.9 oz) yellow onion, chopped

4 cloves garlic, minced

2 large (128 g/4.5 oz) celery stalks, sliced

2 cups (480 ml) chicken stock (page 28) or bone broth (page 44)

¼ cup (60 ml) coconut aminos

1 tablespoon (15 g/0.5 oz) sriracha hot sauce

14.1 ounces (400 g) canned chopped tomatoes

SUGGESTED SIDES:

3 medium (600 g/1.3 lb) turnips, peeled and diced

1 medium (500 g/1.1 lb) savoy cabbage, sliced and core removed

Instructions

Preheat a 5- to 6-quart (4.7- to 5.7-L) slow cooker. Season the meat with salt and pepper. Grease a large heavy-based saucepan or Dutch oven with half of the ghee. Brown the oxtails on all sides and transfer to the slow cooker. Season the cut sides of the marrowbones with salt and pepper and brown on each side for a minute. Crisp up the chicken breasts skin-side down for about 5 minutes, and add to the slow cooker. Finally, add the liver.

Grease the saucepan with the remaining ghee. Add the onion and cook over medium-high heat for 5 to 8 minutes, until lightly browned. Add the garlic, celery, chicken stock, coconut aminos, sriracha, and tomatoes. Bring to a boil, scraping the browned bits off the bottom. Pour into the slow cooker over the meat, cover with a lid, and cook on high for 4 hours or on low for 8 hours.

When done, strain the juices and use them for cooking low-carb vegetable sides (see page 21). To store, shred the meat off the bones, and refrigerate for up to 4 days or freeze for up to 3 months. You can reuse the bones for bone broth (page 44).

NUTRITION FACTS PER SERVING (WITHOUT SUGGESTED SIDES):
Total carbs: 5.5 g / Fiber: 1.1 g / Net carbs: 4.4 g / Protein: 39.3 g / Fat: 30.5 g / Energy: 462 kcal
Macronutrient ratio: Calories from carbs (4%), protein (35%), fat (61%)

Greek Stifado

One thing's for sure: Greeks know their way around the kitchen. This popular dish is proof: It's served in almost every Greek tavern, and it features beef cooked in a rich tomato-and-red-wine sauce that's enhanced by fragrant oregano and warming spices, like cloves, nutmeg, and allspice.

Ingredients

2 pounds (900 g) beef chuck
¾ teaspoon fine sea salt, or to taste
Ground black pepper
¼ cup (55 g/1.9 oz) ghee or other healthy cooking fat (see page 14), divided
1 small (70 g/2.5 oz) yellow onion, chopped
2 cloves garlic, minced
1½ cups (360 ml) dry red wine (see page 31 for substitutions)
¼ cup (60 ml) red wine vinegar
1 cup (240 g/8.5) canned chopped tomatoes
1 tablespoon (15 g/0.5 oz) unsweetened tomato paste
2 bay leaves
2 teaspoons dried oregano
¼ teaspoon ground cinnamon
¼ teaspoon ground allspice
¼ teaspoon ground cloves
⅛ teaspoon ground nutmeg
1.3 pounds (600 g) baby turnips, halved, or regular turnips, diced
Fresh herbs for garnish (basil, oregano, or parsley)

Instructions

Preheat the slow cooker. Cut the beef into large (about 1½-inch/4-cm) chunks and season with salt and pepper. To brown the beef, grease a large heavy-based saucepan or Dutch oven with half of the ghee. Cook the beef in batches until browned on all sides and transfer to the slow cooker.

Grease the saucepan with the remaining ghee. Add the onion and cook over medium-high heat for 5 to 8 minutes, until lightly browned. Add the garlic and cook for a minute. Add the red wine, wine vinegar, tomatoes, tomato paste, bay leaves, oregano, cinnamon, allspice, cloves, and nutmeg. Bring to a boil, scraping the browned bits off the bottom. Pour into the slow cooker over the beef, cover with a lid, and cook on low for 8 hours.

Add the turnips in the last 2 to 3 hours of the cooking process, and stir to combine with the meat and juices. When done, remove the bay leaves, garnish with fresh herbs, and serve. To store, let it cool, and refrigerate for up to 4 days or freeze for up to 3 months.

NUTRITION FACTS PER SERVING:
Total carbs: 11.8 g / Fiber: 2.9 g / Net carbs: 8.9 g / Protein: 30.4 g / Fat: 36.4 g / Energy: 543 kcal
Macronutrient ratio: Calories from carbs (7%), protein (25%), fat (68%)

Spaghetti Squash Bolognese

MAKES: 6 servings
PREPARATION TIME: 25 minutes
COOKING TIME: 4 hours

Spaghetti squash is a great low-carb alternative to traditional pasta, and it's more nutritious, too, because it sports potassium, vitamin A, and B vitamins, plus a significant amount of dietary fiber. And its mild flavor makes it the perfect vehicle for hearty meat sauce made with keto-friendly marinara.

Ingredients

- 5 cups (775 g/1.7 lb) cooked spaghetti squash (see page 19)
- 2 tablespoons (30 g/1.1 oz) ghee or other healthy cooking fat (see page 14), divided
- 4 slices bacon (120 g/4.2 oz), chopped
- 1 small (70 g/2.5 oz) yellow onion, sliced
- 2 cloves garlic, minced
- 1.76 pounds (800 g) minced beef
- 1 recipe marinara sauce (page 25)
- ¼ cup (60 g/2.1 oz) Red Pesto (page 37)
- 1 teaspoon dried oregano
- ¼ teaspoon celery seed
- Fresh basil for garnish
- Optional: ½ cup (45 g/1.6 oz) grated Parmesan cheese

Instructions

Prepare the spaghetti squash by following the instructions on page 19. Heat a large casserole dish greased with 1 tablespoon (15 g) of the ghee over medium heat. Once hot, add the bacon. Cook for about 10 minutes, turning occasionally, until crisped. Use a slotted spoon to transfer the bacon to a plate and set aside.

Grease the saucepan with the remaining 1 tablespoon (15 g) ghee. Add the onion and cook over medium-high heat for 5 to 8 minutes, until lightly browned. Add the garlic and cook for a minute. Add the beef and cook until browned on all sides, 5 to 8 minutes. Add the marinara sauce, pesto, oregano, and celery seed. Bring to a boil. Cook over medium heat for 5 minutes, and take off the heat. Serve with the cooked spaghetti squash (about ¾ cup/130 g/4.6 oz per serving). Top with fresh basil, and optionally, sprinkle with Parmesan cheese. To store, let it cool, and refrigerate for up to 4 days or freeze the meat sauce for up to 3 months.

TIP: Substitute the ground beef, onion, and garlic with an equivalent amount of Make-Ahead Freezer Meatballs (page 45). Cook them in the marinara sauce, covered with a lid, over low heat for 20 to 25 minutes.

NUTRITION FACTS PER SERVING:
Total carbs: 13.9 g / Fiber: 3.3 g / Net carbs: 10.6 g / Protein: 21.9 g / Fat: 42.7 g / Energy: 523 kcal
Macronutrient ratio: Calories from carbs (8%), protein (17%), fat (75%)

Moussaka

Laced with a simple, homemade béchamel sauce, this slow-cooker moussaka is the very best low-carb version of everyone's favorite Greek casserole.

Ingredients

MOUSSAKA:

2 medium (680 kg/1.5 lb) eggplants

1 medium (400 g/14.1 oz) rutabaga, peeled

1½ teaspoons fine sea salt, or to taste

2 tablespoons (30 g/1.1 oz) ghee or other healthy cooking fat (see page 14)

1 small (70 g/2.5 oz) yellow onion, chopped

2 cloves garlic, minced

2.2 pounds (1 kg) ground lamb

3 tablespoons (12 g/0.4 oz) freshly chopped oregano or 1 tablespoon dried oregano

3 tablespoons (12 g/0.4 oz) freshly chopped mint or 1 tablespoon dried mint

1 teaspoon ground cinnamon

½ teaspoon ground cloves

1 bay leaf, crumbled

¼ teaspoon ground black pepper

2 tablespoons (30 g/1.1 oz) unsweetened tomato paste

1 cup (240 ml) dry red wine (see page 31 for substitutions)

Instructions

Preheat the slow cooker and grease with a small amount of ghee. Cut the eggplant and rutabaga into about ¼-inch (½-cm) slices. Season the eggplant and rutabaga slices with salt, and set aside for 20 minutes. Pat dry any excess moisture off the eggplant using a paper towel.

Meanwhile, grease a large heavy-based saucepan or Dutch oven with the ghee. Add the onion and cook over medium-high heat for 5 to 8 minutes, until lightly browned. Add the garlic and cook for a minute. Add the lamb and cook over medium heat until browned on all sides, about 5 minutes, stirring frequently. Add the oregano, mint, cinnamon, cloves, bay leaf, black pepper, tomato paste, and red wine. Cook for 5 to 8 minutes, or until the sauce is reduced by half. Season to taste and set aside.

To assemble the moussaka, place a layer of the rutabaga slices on the bottom of the slow cooker. Add a layer of eggplant slices (about a third of the amount), and half of the meat mixture. Add another third of rutabaga-eggplant slices and the remaining meat mixture. Top with the remaining rutabaga-eggplant slices. Cover with a lid and cook on low for 8 hours.

In the meantime, prepare the béchamel sauce. In a saucepan, mix the cream, egg yolks, nutmeg, and crumbled bay leaf. Cook over medium-low heat, stirring constantly, until it starts to thicken. Take off the heat and mix in 1 cup (90 g/3.2 oz) of the grated Parmesan cheese. After 6 hours of cooking the moussaka, pour in the béchamel sauce. Sprinkle with the

NUTRITION FACTS PER SERVING:
Total carbs: 14.7 g / Fiber: 4.7 g / Net carbs: 10 g / Protein: 31.4 g / Fat: 52.8 g / Energy: 685 kcal
Macronutrient ratio: Calories from carbs (6%), protein (20%), fat (74%)

BÉCHAMEL SAUCE:

1½ cups (360 ml) heavy whipping cream

4 egg yolks

¼ teaspoon ground nutmeg

1 bay leaf, crumbled

1½ cups (135 g/4.8 oz) grated Parmesan cheese, divided

Salt and pepper

remaining ½ cup (45 g) Parmesan cheese, cover with a lid, and cook for another 2 hours. Optionally, you can crisp the moussaka in the oven at 400°F (200°C, or gas mark 6) for 5 to 8 minutes, or until the top is golden brown. Serve immediately, or let it cool and refrigerate for up to 4 days or freeze for up to 3 months.

Korean Beef & Kimchi Stew

If you've never tried kimchi—that is, Korean fermented cabbage—before, this stew is the place to start: kimchi is responsible for its amazing depth of flavor and slow-burning heat. Serve it over cauli-rce (page 18) that's been cooked in the beef's juices. You'll fall in love with it.

Ingredients

STEW:

2 pounds (900 g) beef chuck

½ teaspoon fine sea salt, or to taste

½ teaspoon ground black pepper, plus more for seasoning the beef

3 tablespoons (45 g/1.6 oz) ghee or other healthy cooking fat (see page 14), divided

1 small (70 g/2.5 oz) yellow onion, chopped

3 cloves garlic, minced

1 cup (240 ml) bone broth (page 44) or beef stock

2 tablespoons (30 ml) rice wine or white wine vinegar

2 tablespoons (30 ml) coconut aminos

2 bay leaves

½ teaspoon coarse Korean red pepper

1.3 pounds (600 g) kimchi (make your own, page 26)

Suggested side: cauli-rice (page 18)

GARNISH:

2 tablespoons (30 ml) toasted sesame oil

2 tablespoons (18 g/0.6 oz) sesame seeds

2 medium (30 g/1.1 oz) spring onions, sliced

Instructions

Preheat the slow cooker. Cut the beef into 1½-inch (4-cm) chunks, and season with salt and pepper. To brown the beef, grease a large heavy-based saucepan or Dutch oven with half of the ghee. Cook the beef in batches until browned on all sides and transfer to the slow cooker.

Grease the saucepan with the remaining ghee. Add the onion and cook over medium-high heat for 5 to 8 minutes, until lightly browned. Add the garlic and cook for a minute. Pour in the bone broth, rice wine, and coconut aminos. Bring to a boil, scraping the browned bits off the bottom. Pour into the slow cooker over the browned beef. Add the bay leaves, ½ teaspoon of black pepper, Korean red pepper, and kimchi. Stir to combine, cover with a lid, and cook for 4 hours on high or for 8 hours on low.

If serving with cauli-rice, ladle 1 to 2 cups (120 to 240 ml) of the cooking juices from the slow cooker into a saucepan with uncooked cauliflower rice, and cook for 5 to 8 minutes over medium heat.

To serve, drizzle with the sesame oil and sprinkle with the sesame seeds and spring onion. To store, let it cool, and refrigerate for up to 4 days or freeze for up to 3 months.

NUTRITION FACTS PER SERVING (WITHOUT SUGGESTED SIDE):
Total carbs: 6.9 g / Fiber: 2.7 g / Net carbs: 4.2 g / Protein: 32.1 g / Fat: 41.1 g / Energy: 540 kcal
Macronutrient ratio: Calories from carbs (3%), protein (25%), fat (72%)

Reuben Meatloaf

Best served with roasted Brussels sprouts or coleslaw, this slow-cooker-friendly meatloaf is basically a huge low-carb Reuben-style sandwich. Drizzle it with homemade Russian dressing, and it's irresistible.

Ingredients

MEATLOAF:

2 tablespoons (30 g/1.1 oz) ghee or other healthy cooking fat (see page 14)

1 medium (110 g/3.9 oz) yellow onion, chopped

2 pounds (900 g) ground beef

½ teaspoon fine sea salt

2 tablespoons (30 g/1.1 oz) unsweetened tomato paste

1 tablespoon (15 g/0.5 oz) Dijon mustard

1 teaspoon caraway seeds

1 large egg, lightly beaten

2 cups (284 g/10 oz) sauerkraut, drained (make your own, page 25)

⅓ cup (40 g/1.6 oz) coconut flour

8.8 ounces (250 g) slices beef pastrami, divided

1½ cups (180 g/6.4 oz) grated Swiss cheese such as Gruyère, divided

Suggested side: (2.76 lb) 1.25 kg Brussels sprouts, trimmed and halved (optional)

Instructions

Grease a large heavy-based saucepan or Dutch oven with the ghee. Add the onion and cook over medium-high heat for 5 to 8 minutes, or until lightly browned. Set aside.

Preheat the oven to 350°F (175°C, or gas mark 4). In a bowl, mix the beef, salt, tomato paste, Dijon mustard, caraway seeds, egg, sauerkraut, and coconut flour. Mix until well combined, place on a piece of heavy-duty baking foil, and flatten the meat mixture into a large rectangle (no larger than your baking tray). Lay half of the pastrami slices vertically in a single layer. Top with half of the grated cheese. Roll up the meatloaf starting from the short side up, peeling the foil while rolling, and finish with the seam side down.

Transfer to a baking dish, keeping the baking foil under the meatloaf. Bake uncovered for 30 minutes. After 30 minutes, lay the remaining pastrami slices on top of the meatloaf and sprinkle with the remaining grated cheese. Place in the oven, increase the temperature to 400°F (200°C, or gas mark 6), and bake for about 10 minutes, or until the cheese is melted and an instant-read thermometer inserted into the thickest part registers 160°F (71°C).

In the meantime, prepare the Russian dressing by mixing all the ingredients and set aside. When done, let the meatloaf cool for 5 to 10 minutes before slicing. Optionally, you can add

NUTRITION FACTS PER SERVING (WITHOUT SUGGESTED SIDE):
Total carbs: 5.4 g / Fiber: 2.3 g / Net carbs: 3.1 g / Protein: 29.4 g / Fat: 39 g / Energy: 493 kcal
Macronutrient ratio: Calories from carbs (3%), protein (24%), fat (73%)

RUSSIAN DRESSING:

½ cup (110 g/3.9 oz) mayonnaise (make your own, page 25)

¼ cup (58 g/2 oz) full-fat sour cream

1 tablespoon (15 g/0.5 oz) sriracha chili sauce

2 medium (112 g/4 oz) pickled cucumbers

2 teaspoons (10 g/0.4 oz) freshly grated horseradish or horseradish paste

3 tablespoons (45 ml) fresh lemon juice

3 tablespoons (12 g/0.4 oz) freshly chopped parsley

3 tablespoons (9 g/0.3 oz) freshly chopped chives

Salt and pepper

Brussels sprouts for the last 15 to 20 minutes of the cooking process. Season them with salt and pepper, and coat them in the cooking juices. Serve immediately, or let it cool and refrigerate for up to 4 days or freeze for up to 3 months.

TIP: To make this meatloaf in a slow cooker, halve the recipe and cook the meatloaf on low for 6 to 8 hours. If you're using Brussels sprouts, add them in the last 2 hours of the cooking process.

MAKES: 8 servings
PREPARATION TIME: 20 minutes
COOKING TIME: 30 minutes

Pepperoni Cauli-Pizza Casserole

When you need a pizza fix in a hurry, you don't have time to mess around with making crusts. That's where this casserole comes in; it's a simplified (yet equally delicious!) version of classic low-carb cauliflower pizza.

Ingredients

2 medium (1.25 kg/2.76 lb) cauliflowers, cut into florets
1 recipe marinara sauce (page 25)
3.5 ounces (100 g) pepperoni slices
1 cup (240 g/8.5 oz) full-fat cream cheese, at room temperature
1 jalapeño pepper (14 g/0.5 oz), sliced
1 teaspoon dried oregano
¼ to ½ teaspoon red pepper flakes
2 cups (226 g/8 oz) shredded mozzarella cheese, divided
1 cup (90 g/3.2 oz) grated Parmesan cheese, divided
Salt and pepper
Fresh basil for garnish

Instructions

Preheat the oven to 400°F (200°C, or gas mark 6). Steam the cauliflower for 5 to 8 minutes, or until crisp-tender. Drain and place in a large casserole dish or an ovenproof skillet.

In the meantime, prepare the marinara sauce (page 25). Slice the pepperoni and leave 10 to 15 whole slices for topping. Mix the marinara sauce with the cream cheese and pour over the cooked cauliflower. Add the jalapeño pepper, pepperoni, oregano, pepper flakes, grated mozzarella and Parmesan (reserve some grated cheeses for topping). Mix until well combined, and season with salt and pepper to taste. Top with the reserved cheeses and the pepperoni slices, and transfer to the oven. Bake for 15 to 18 minutes, or until the top is lightly browned and crispy. When done, remove from the oven and let it cool for a few minutes before slicing. Garnish with fresh basil. Serve immediately, or let it cool and refrigerate for up to 5 days or freeze for up to 3 months.

NUTRITION FACTS PER SERVING:
Total carbs: 12.8 g / Fiber: 3.9 g / Net carbs: 8.9 g / Protein: 19.8 g / Fat: 29.1 g / Energy: 369 kcal
Macronutrient ratio: Calories from carbs (9%), protein (21%), fat (70%)

BBQ Pulled Pork Sliders

Rich, tender, juicy pulled pork is at its best when paired with a punchy side dish like spicy, homemade coleslaw. Add a couple of Sourdough Keto Buns (page 52), and you've got genuine low-carb soul food.

Ingredients

SPICE RUB:

1 tablespoon ground cumin

1 teaspoon garlic powder

1 teaspoon onion powder

1 teaspoon paprika

1 teaspoon chili powder

1 teaspoon mustard powder

½ teaspoon ground black pepper

1½ teaspoons fine sea salt

PORK SLIDERS:

3.3 pounds (1.5 kg) bone-in pork shoulder or 2.65 pounds (1.2 kg) boneless pork shoulder

¼ cup (60 ml) water

¾ cup (180 g/6.4 oz) Sweet & Sour BBQ sauce (page 42)

Suggestions (per serving): 1 or 2 mini Sourdough Keto Buns (page 52)

SPICY SLAW:

1 pound (450 g) green cabbage, shredded

1 small (60 g/2.1 oz) red onion, sliced

1 piece (14 g/0.5 oz) jalapeño pepper, chopped

⅓ cup (73/2.6 oz) mayonnaise (page 25)

3 tablespoons (45 ml) fresh lime juice

1 teaspoon Dijon mustard

¼ teaspoon red pepper flakes

2 tablespoons (8 g/0.3 oz) freshly chopped cilantro or parsley

Salt and pepper

Instructions

Preheat the slow cooker. Prepare the rub by mixing all the spices. Pat dry the pork using a paper towel and cover in the spice rub, pressing it all over and cover in plastic wrap, refrigerate, and let it marinate for 8 hours or up to 24 hours. (If you're short on time, marinating can be skipped.) Transfer to the slow cooker, add the water, and cook on high for 4 to 5 hours, until the meat is tender.

Prepare the spicy slaw by mixing all the ingredients: cabbage, red onion, jalapeño pepper, mayonnaise, lime juice, Dijon mustard, pepper flakes, cilantro, and salt and pepper to taste. Cover and refrigerate to let the flavors combine.

When the meat is cooked, shred it with two forks. Add the BBQ sauce and combine with the cooking juices. Serve the pork with the prepared slaw, and optionally with the buns. Keep leftovers refrigerated for up to 4 days, or freeze for up to 3 months.

NUTRITION FACTS PER SERVING (WITHOUT KETO BUNS):
Total carbs: 7.3 g / Fiber: 2.5 g / Net carbs: 4.8 g / Protein: 27.3 g / Fat: 36.6 g / Energy: 468 kcal
Macronutrient ratio: Calories from carbs (4%), protein (24%), fat (72%)

BBQ Pork Ribs

Slow-cooking these pork ribs ensures that they're extra-tender; drenching them in a sugar-free mole barbeque sauce and roasting them in the oven afterwards adds dark, bewitching flavor. The result? A melt-in-the-mouth wonder.

Ingredients

MARINATED RIBS:

2 tablespoons (14 g/0.5 oz) smoked paprika or ancho chile powder

1 tablespoon (9 g/0.3 oz) mustard powder

2 teaspoons ground cumin

1 teaspoon celery seeds

1 teaspoon garlic powder

1 teaspoon ground black pepper

2 teaspoons fine sea salt

¼ cup (40 g/1.4 oz) brown sugar substitute such as Sukrin, erythritol, or Swerve

4 pounds (1.8 kg) pork spare ribs, will yield about 50% meat

Suggested side: coleslaw (page 141)

BBQ SAUCE:

Use ½ cup (120 g/4.2 oz) Sweet & Sour BBQ Sauce (page 42), or try the following variation by mixing these ingredients:

¼ cup (60 g/2.1 oz) Sweet & Sour BBQ Sauce (page 42)

1 heaping tablespoon (30 g/1.1 oz) Cranberry Sauce (page 43)

1 tablespoon (15 ml) coconut or apple cider vinegar

1 tablespoon (15 ml) coconut aminos

1 tablespoons (5 g/0.2 oz) cocoa powder

Instructions

Preheat the slow cooker and pour in ¼ cup (60 ml) of water. Prepare the rub by mixing all the spices and set aside. Pat dry the ribs using a paper towel and cover them in the spice rub, pressing it all over the ribs. Place the ribs in plastic wrap, refrigerate, and let them marinate for 8 hours or up to 24 hours. (If you're short on time, marinating can be skipped.) Transfer them to the slow cooker and cook on high for 4 to 5 hours, until the meat is tender.

When done, use tongs to carefully remove the ribs from the slow cooker and place them on a baking sheet lined with heavy-duty parchment paper. Preheat the broiler. Brush the BBQ sauce on both sides of the pork ribs and place under the broiler. Cook for 8 to 10 minutes, turning halfway through. Serve the ribs with coleslaw (page 141) or other low-carb veggie sides (page 21).

NUTRITION FACTS PER SERVING (WITHOUT SUGGESTED SIDE):
Total carbs: 4.8 g / Fiber: 1.9 g / Net carbs: 2.9 g / Protein: 24.5 g / Fat: 37 g / Energy: 451 kcal
Macronutrient ratio: Calories from carbs (3%), protein (22%), fat (75%)

Sausage & Cabbage Stew

It takes just fifteen minutes of hands-on time to prepare this simple German-style sausage stew; then you can sit back and let your slow cooker take over. A few hours later, you'll be rewarded with a satisfying, one-bowl meal that's heavy on healthy veggies, like shredded cabbage, celeriac, and sauerkraut.

Ingredients

BOUQUET GARNI:

2 sprigs fresh parsley

2 sprigs fresh thyme

1 teaspoon peppercorns

3 whole allspice

2 bay leaves

STEW:

¼ cup (55 g/1.9 oz) ghee or other healthy cooking fat (see page 14), divided

1.76 pounds (800 g) kielbasa or gluten-free Italian-style sausages

1 small (70 g/2.5 oz) yellow onion, chopped

½ small (150 g/5.3 oz) celeriac, peeled and diced

2 cloves garlic, minced

1 medium (600 g/1.3 lb) head green cabbage, shredded and core removed

1 cup (142 g/5 oz) sauerkraut, drained (make your own, page 25)

½ teaspoon fine sea salt, or to taste

1 cup (240 ml) bone broth (page 44) or chicken stock (page 28)

1 tablespoon freshly chopped parsley

Instructions

Preheat the slow cooker. Make the bouquet garni by placing all the herbs in a piece of cheesecloth and tying with unwaxed kitchen string.

Grease a large heavy-based skillet or Dutch oven with half of the ghee. Add the sausages and brown for 1 to 2 minutes on both sides. Transfer to a plate and set aside.

Grease the skillet with the remaining ghee. Add the onion and cook over medium-high heat for 5 to 8 minutes, until lightly browned. Add the celeriac and garlic. Cook for a minute, until fragrant.

Transfer to the slow cooker. Add the cabbage, sauerkraut, bouquet garni, salt, and bone broth, and combine well. Top with the browned sausages, and cover with a lid. Cook on high for 3 hours or on low for 6 hours. When done, remove the bouquet garni and garnish with parsley. Eat immediately, or let it cool, and refrigerate for up to 4 days or freeze for up to 3 months.

NUTRITION FACTS PER SERVING:
Total carbs: 11.9 g / Fiber: 4.6 g / Net carbs: 7.3 g / Protein: 24.5 g / Fat: 33.6 g / Energy: 437 kcal
Macronutrient ratio: Calories from carbs (7%), protein (23%), fat (70%)

Pork Pot Roast with Vegetables

Pot roast is traditionally made with beef, but it works just as well (if not better!) with pork: pop a juicy, spice-rubbed pork shoulder into your Dutch oven, and you'll get perfectly cooked meat with deliciously crispy skin.

Ingredients

SPICE RUB:

1 tablespoon (10 g/0.3 oz) garlic powder

1 tablespoon (7 g/0.2 oz) onion powder

1 tablespoon (5 g/0.2 oz) dried oregano

½ teaspoon fennel seeds

1½ teaspoons fine sea salt

1 teaspoon ground black pepper

POT ROAST:

2.65 pounds (1.2 kg) pork shoulder, boneless

3 tablespoons (45 g/1.6 oz) ghee or other healthy cooking fat (see page 14), divided

2 bay leaves

1½ cups (360 ml) water, plus more if needed

1 medium (110 g/3.9 oz) yellow onion, sliced

3 large (192 g/6.8 oz) celery stalks, sliced

4 medium (800 g/1.76 lb) turnips or kohlrabi, cut into 1-inch (2.5-cm) cubes, and/or halved baby turnips

10.6 ounces (300 g) dark-leaf kale, chopped and stems removed

Instructions

Prepare the rub by mixing all the spices. Pat dry the pork using a paper towel and cover in the spice rub, pressing it all over. Place in plastic wrap, refrigerate, and let it marinate for 8 hours or up to 24 hours. (If you're short on time, marinating can be skipped.)

Preheat the oven to 350°F (175°C, or gas mark 4). Grease a large heavy-based saucepan or Dutch oven with half the ghee. Sear the marinated pork roast in the saucepan on all sides until the spice coating is golden brown, about 1 minute per side. Transfer to a deep casserole dish, and add the bay leaves and 1 cup (240 ml) of the water. Cover with a lid and cook for 3 hours.

In the meantime, grease a large heavy-based saucepan or Dutch oven with the remaining ghee. Add the onion and cook over medium-high heat for 5 to 8 minutes, until lightly browned. Add the celery, remaining ½ cup (120 ml) water, turnips, and kale. Cook for 1 to 2 minutes, until the kale is wilted. Take off the heat and set aside.

After 3 hours of cooking, remove the casserole dish from the oven. Add the browned vegetables, cover with a lid, and put back in the oven. Cook covered for 1 hour or until the vegetables are tender. When done, remove from the oven and set aside for 5 to 10 minutes. Discard the bay leaves and serve, or let it cool and refrigerate for up to 4 days or freeze for up to 3 months.

NUTRITION FACTS PER SERVING:
Total carbs: 12.3 g / Fiber: 4.3 g / Net carbs: 8 g / Protein: 28.6 g / Fat: 33.4 g / Energy: 465 kcal
Macronutrient ratio: Calories from carbs (7%), protein (26%), fat (67%)

Pork & Kohlrabi Stew

My mom used to make this stew with homegrown kohlrabi when I was a kid, and I just loved it. So I came up with this low-carb version, which has the added bonus of being exceptionally rich in potassium and magnesium—and that means it's your secret weapon against keto-flu!

Ingredients

- 1.3 pounds (600 g) pork shoulder, boneless
- 1 teaspoon fine sea salt, or to taste
- Freshly ground black pepper
- 2 tablespoons (30 g/1.1 oz) ghee or other healthy cooking fat (see page 14)
- 2 teaspoons paprika
- 2 teaspoons onion powder
- ½ teaspoon caraway seeds
- ⅛ teaspoon ground allspice
- 3 cups (720 ml) bone broth (page 44) or vegetable stock or chicken stock (page 28)
- 2 medium (600 g/1.3 lb) kohlrabi or turnips
- 2 medium (400 g/0.9 lb) zucchini, sliced
- 4 egg yolks
- ½ cup (120 ml) heavy whipping cream or coconut milk
- 2 tablespoons freshly chopped parsley or chives

Instructions

Using a paper towel, pat dry the pork, and season with salt and pepper on both sides. Cut into medium-large chunks, 1 to 1½ inches (2 to 4 cm) thick. Grease a large heavy-bottom pot or Dutch oven with the ghee and heat over medium-high heat. Once hot, add the pork, paprika, onion powder, caraway, allspice, and 1 teaspoon salt. Cook over medium-high heat for a few minutes, until browned on all sides. Pour in the broth and bring to a boil. Once boiling, reduce the heat to low and cover with a lid. Cook for 1 hour and 15 minutes, or until the pork is tender. Check every 20 minutes and add water if needed.

Peel and slice the kohlrabi and zucchini into ½-inch (1-cm) thick pieces. Once the pork is tender, add the kohlrabi and cover with a lid. Cook until tender, 25 to 30 minutes. Add the the zucchini and cook for another 10 minutes.

Finally, prepare the "egg yolk thickener." Whisk the egg yolks with the cream. When the zucchini is tender, slowly pour in the thickener mixture while stirring. Cook for about a minute, and turn off the heat. Season with salt and pepper, and add the parsley or chives. Serve warm, or let it cool, and refrigerate for up to 4 days or freeze for up to 3 months.

TIP: If using a slow cooker, double the recipe. Place everything—apart from the kohlrabi and zucchini—in the slow cooker. Cook on high for 4 to 5 hours. Add the sliced kohlrabi and zucchini in the last 2 hours of the cooking process. Lastly, slowly stir in the egg yolk–cream to thicken the sauce.

NUTRITION FACTS PER SERVING:
Total carbs: 15.7 g / Fiber: 7.1 g / Net carbs: 8.6 g / Protein: 39.2 g / Fat: 39.2 g / Energy: 571 kcal
Macronutrient ratio: Calories from carbs (6%), protein (29%), fat (65%)

Crispy Chinese Pork Belly

Salting is the best way to create perfectly crispy pork belly, because it draws moisture from the skin and helps it become crisp. (Just don't use fine salt, or the result will be too salty.) Serve warm with Sweet & Sour BBQ Sauce (page 42) and cooked greens.

Ingredients

- 2.65 pounds (1.2 kg) boneless pork belly
- 1 teaspoon Chinese five spice
- 1 teaspoon fine sea salt
- ½ teaspoon ground black or white pepper
- 2 cloves garlic, crushed
- 2 tablespoons (30 ml) Chinese rice wine (Shaoxing)
- ¼ cup (60 ml) coconut aminos
- 2 teaspoons rice wine vinegar or coconut vinegar
- 1 cup (250 g/8.8 oz) coarse sea salt, or enough to cover the skin

Instructions

Rinse and pat dry the pork belly. Using a skewer, prick the skin, creating many tiny holes all over it, or you can use a meat tenderizer specifically for this purpose. The more tiny holes you create, the puffier the skin will get. Do not pierce the skin all the way to the fat or meat layer. If you skip this step, the skin will still be crispy but it won't be puffy.

Mix the Chinese five spice, salt, and pepper. Rub it into the flesh—but not the skin. Place the garlic, rice wine, and coconut aminos in a container that will fit in the fridge. Place the pork belly in the container, skin-side up. Rub the marinade on the sides—but not the skin. Place in the fridge and marinate uncovered for 8 to 24 hours.

Remove the marinated pork belly from the fridge and let it sit for 15 to 20 minutes. Preheat the oven to 350°F (175°C, or gas mark 4). Discard the marinade. Place the pork belly skin-side up on a large piece of foil and fold all four sides up around the pork belly until it is snug, creating a tight rim around it. Brush the skin with the vinegar and spread the coarse salt on top—not the sides. Place in the oven and bake for 1 hour 15 minutes to 1 hour 30 minutes (if the cut is thick or bone is attached).

Remove the tray from the oven, place on a cooling rack, and switch to broil at 440°F (225°C). Remove the salt crust and brush any excess salt off the top of the pork. Discard the foil and juices, and place the pork belly on a rack inside a baking tray. Move the oven rack to the lowest position and cook for 15 to 20 minutes, until the skin is puffy and golden brown. When done, remove the tray from the oven and let the

NUTRITION FACTS PER SERVING:
Total carbs: 1 g / Fiber: 0.1 g / Net carbs: 0.9 g / Protein: 14 g / Fat: 45 g / Energy: 447 kcal
Macronutrient ratio: Calories from carbs (1%), protein (12%), fat (87%)

pork rest for 10 to 15 minutes before slicing. Serve warm with mustard or BBQ sauce and crispy greens or flavored cauli-rice (page 51). Crisped-up pork belly is best served fresh. It can be refrigerated for up to 4 days, but it will lose its crispiness.

Greek Kleftiko

Kleftiko is a rustic dish of tender lamb flavored with lemon and oregano and served with baked vegetables. *Kleftiko* translates as "stolen": according to Greek legend, bandits would steal lamb and goats from grazing flocks and cook them in underground pits to seal in the smoke. This version is so good you'll want to keep it to yourself, too!

Ingredients

MARINATED LAMB:

2 pounds (900 g) boneless leg of lamb, cut into 1½-inch (4-cm) chunks

1 medium (100 g/3.5 oz) red onion, chopped

4 cloves garlic, minced

Zest and juice from 1 lemon

1 tablespoon (5 g/0.2 oz) dried oregano

1 tablespoon (15 g/0.5 oz) Dijon mustard

¼ cup (60 ml) extra-virgin olive oil

¾ teaspoon fine sea salt, or to taste

Ground black pepper

STEW:

1 medium (400 g/14.1 oz) rutabaga, peeled and cut into 1-inch (2.5-cm) pieces

2 medium (240 g/8.5 oz) green bell peppers, cut into chunks

1 large (240 g/8.5 oz) tomato, diced (or use canned diced tomatoes)

Optional: 8 ounces (225 g) diced halloumi

Fresh parsley, oregano, or basil for garnish

Instructions

Place the lamb in a bowl and add all the ingredients for the marinade: red onion, garlic, lemon zest and juice, oregano, Dijon mustard, olive oil, salt, and pepper. Combine well, cover, and refrigerate for 2 hours or up to 12 hours.

Preheat the oven to 300°F (150°C, or gas mark 2). Place all the ingredients from the bowl into a large casserole dish. Add the rutabaga, green peppers, and tomato. Combine all the ingredients, cover with a lid or foil, and transfer to the oven. Bake for 3 hours 40 minutes, and remove the lid. Add the halloumi (if using) and bake for another 20 minutes. When done, remove from the oven and let it rest for 10 to 15 minutes. Garnish with fresh herbs and serve immediately. To store, let it cool, and refrigerate for up to 4 days or freeze for up to 3 months.

NUTRITION FACTS PER SERVING:
Total carbs: 12.2 g / Fiber: 3.4 g / Net carbs: 8.8 g / Protein: 29.3 g / Fat: 32.3 g / Energy: 458 kcal
Macronutrient ratio: Calories from carbs (8%), protein (26%), fat (66%)

Lamb Rogan Josh

This delectable, mildly spicy curry is a staple of Kashmiri cuisine. It's made with sweet tomatoes, warming chiles, and stimulating, aromatic spices like cardamom and cinnamon. If you like yours on the spicy side, add some chili powder for extra heat.

Ingredients

2.65 pounds (1.2 kg) boneless leg of lamb

Salt and pepper

¼ cup (55 g/1.9 oz) ghee or other healthy cooking fat (see page 14), divided

1 medium (110 g/3.9 oz) yellow onion, chopped

1 recipe Rogan Josh Curry Paste (page 23)

2 large (400 g/7.1 oz) tomatoes, diced (or use canned diced tomatoes)

1 cup (240 ml) bone broth (page 44) or vegetable stock (page 28)

2 bay leaves

1 cup (230 g/8.1 oz) full-fat sour cream or creamed coconut milk (see page 27)

Optional: ⅔ cup (60 g/2.1 oz) toasted flaked almonds and fresh cilantro for topping

Suggested side: cauli-rice (page 18) or shirataki rice (page 19)

Instructions

Preheat the slow cooker. Cut the lamb into 1½-inch (4-cm) chunks, and season with salt and pepper. Grease a large heavy-based saucepan or Dutch oven with half of the ghee. Cook the lamb in batches until browned on all sides and transfer to the slow cooker.

Grease the pan where you cooked the lamb with the remaining ghee. Add the onion and cook over medium-high heat for 5 to 8 minutes, until lightly browned. Add the Rogan Josh curry paste and cook for a minute, stirring frequently. Mix in the tomatoes, bone broth, and bay leaves, and transfer to the slow cooker. Cover with a lid. Cook on low for 8 hours or on high for 4 hours.

When done, discard the bay leaves and mix in the sour cream. Taste and season if needed. Optionally, top with toasted flaked almonds and fresh cilantro, and serve with steamed cauli-rice or shirataki rice. To store, let it cool, and refrigerate for up to 4 days or freeze for up to 3 months.

NUTRITION FACTS PER SERVING:
Total carbs: 7.6 g / Fiber: 2 g / Net carbs: 5.6 g / Protein: 29.7 g / Fat: 36.3 g / Energy: 477 kcal
Macronutrient ratio: Calories from carbs (5%), protein (25%), fat (70%)

Kefta Meatball & Egg Tagine

There's only one way to make this dish of tender, Moroccan-style lamb meatballs better than it already is: finish it by poaching eggs right in its savory, olive-spiked sauce, as with Green Shakshuka (page 83).

Ingredients

MEATBALLS:

14.1 ounces (400 g) ground lamb

2 tablespoons (16 g/0.6 oz) coconut flour or ½ cup (50 g/1.8 oz) almond flour

1 large egg

1 clove garlic, minced

1 teaspoon paprika

½ teaspoon ground cumin

¼ teaspoon ground cinnamon

1 tablespoon (4 g/0.2 oz) freshly chopped parsley

1 tablespoon (4 g/0.2 oz) freshly chopped cilantro

TAGINE:

2 tablespoons (30 g/1.1 oz) ghee or other healthy cooking fat (see page 14)

1 small (70 g/2.5 oz) yellow onion, chopped

1 clove garlic, minced

1 large (240 g/8.5 oz) tomato, diced (or use canned diced tomatoes)

½ cup (120 ml) water

1 medium (250 g/8.8 oz) eggplant, cut into ½-inch (1-cm) pieces

1 teaspoon paprika

½ teaspoon ground cumin

¼ teaspoon ground cinnamon

2 tablespoons (8 g/0.3 oz) freshly chopped parsley, divided

2 tablespoons (8 g/0.3 oz) freshly chopped cilantro, divided

16 whole (48 g/1.7 oz) green pitted olives

4 large eggs

Suggested side: cauli-rice (page 18)

Instructions

In a bowl, mix the lamb, coconut flour, egg, garlic, paprika, cumin, cinnamon, parsley, and cilantro. Using your hands, create 12 medium-size meatballs (about 40 g/1.4 oz each).

Grease a large skillet or casserole dish with the ghee. Add the onion and cook over medium-high heat for 5 to 8 minutes, or until lightly browned. Add the garlic, tomatoes, water, eggplant, paprika, cumin, cinnamon, parsley, and cilantro (reserve some herbs for garnish). Mix until well combined. Add the meatballs and green olives, and bring to a boil. Cover with a lid and simmer over medium-low heat for 15 to 20 minutes.

Remove the lid and use a spoon to make 4 wells. Crack the eggs into the wells, cover with a lid, and cook for another 8 to 10 minutes, or until the egg whites are set and the egg yolks still runny. Serve with plain or flavored cauli-rice (page 51). To store, let it cool, and refrigerate for up to 4 days.

TIP: Using a tagine dish? Preheat the oven to 350°F (175°C, or gas mark 4). Prepare the sauce and pour it into the tagine dish. Add the meatballs and olives, cover with a lid, and bake for 25 to 30 minutes. Crack in the eggs and bake for another 10 minutes, or until the egg whites are set.

NUTRITION FACTS PER SERVING:
Total carbs: 11.2 g / Fiber: 4.6 g / Net carbs: 6.6 g / Protein: 27.5 g / Fat: 37.1 g / Energy: 485 kcal
Macronutrient ratio: Calories from carbs (6%), protein (23%), fat (71%)

Moroccan Lamb Stew

Got a jar of homemade harissa paste (page 39) lingering in the fridge? Crack it open and put it to good use by making a batch of this North African classic, which features spiced lamb, rich broth, and plenty of green olives.

Ingredients

2.65 pounds (1.2 kg) boneless leg of lamb

1 teaspoon fine sea salt, or to taste

Ground black pepper

3 tablespoons (45 g/1.6 oz) ghee or other healthy cooking fat (see page 14), divided

1 small (70 g/2.5 oz) yellow onion, chopped

2 cloves garlic, minced

3 large (192 g/6.8 oz) celery stalks, sliced

2 medium (400 g/7.1 oz) tomatoes, diced (or use canned diced tomatoes)

2 cups (480 ml) bone broth (page 44)

¼ cup (63 g/2.2 oz) coconut butter or almond butter

1 tablespoon (7 g/0.2 oz) paprika

1 tablespoon (7 g/0.2 oz) onion powder

1 teaspoon garlic powder

3 tablespoons (45 g/1.6 oz) harissa paste (page 39)

1 cup (100 g/3.5 oz) pitted green olives

Suggested side: cauli-rice (page 18) or shirataki rice (page 19)

Fresh cilantro or parsley for garnish

Instructions

Preheat the slow cooker. Cut the lamb into 1½-inch (4-cm) chunks, and season with salt and pepper. To brown the lamb, grease a large heavy-based saucepan or Dutch oven with half of the ghee. Cook the lamb in batches until browned on all sides and transfer to the slow cooker.

Grease the pan where you cooked the lamb with the remaining ghee. Add the onion and cook over medium-high heat for 5 to 8 minutes, until lightly browned. Add the garlic, celery, tomatoes, bone broth, and coconut butter, and bring to a boil. Pour into the slow cooker. Add the paprika, onion powder, garlic powder, and harissa paste. Cover with a lid. Cook on low for 8 hours or on high for 4 hours. Stir in the olives in the last 30 to 60 minutes of the cooking process.

When done, taste and season if needed. Serve with steamed cauli-rice or shirataki rice. Garnish with fresh cilantro. To store, let it cool, and refrigerate for up to 4 days or freeze for up to 3 months.

NUTRITION FACTS PER SERVING (WITHOUT SUGGESTED SIDE):
Total carbs: 8.5 g / Fiber: 3.5 g / Net carbs: 5 g / Protein: 30.1 g / Fat: 34.4 g / Energy: 480 kcal
Macronutrient ratio: Calories from carbs (4%), protein (26%), fat (70%)

Leg of Lamb with Mint & Green Beans

With just a few basic ingredients, this pared-down meal couldn't be simpler—or more elegant. After hours in the slow cooker, the meat is fall-off-the-bone tender, and it's a great counterpoint to the crisp green beans.

Ingredients

3.3 pounds (1.5 kg) bone-in lamb leg, will yield about 50% meat

½ teaspoon salt, or more to taste

Freshly ground black pepper

2 tablespoons (30 g/1.1 oz) ghee or other healthy cooking fat (see page 14)

4 cloves garlic, sliced

3 to 4 tablespoons (12 to 16 g) freshly chopped mint or 1 tablespoon dried mint

¼ cup (60 ml) water

1.3 pounds (600 g) green beans, trimmed

Instructions

Preheat the slow cooker. Using a paper towel, pat dry the lamb, and season with salt and pepper. Grease a large pot with the ghee. Place the lamb in the pot and fry until golden brown on all sides. When done, take off the heat and set aside.

Make small incisions into the lamb using a knife, and press in the garlic slices. Place the lamb in the slow cooker and sprinkle with the mint. Add the water, cover with a lid, and cook on low for 8 hours.

After 6 hours of cooking, transfer the lamb to a plate. Place the green beans in the slow cooker and add back the lamb. Cook for another 2 hours, or until the green beans are crisp-tender and the meat is soft and juicy. To store, let it cool, and refrigerate for up to 4 days or freeze for up to 3 months.

NUTRITION FACTS PER SERVING:
Total carbs: 12 g / Fiber: 4.4 g / Net carbs: 7.6 g / Protein: 37.3 g / Fat: 36.4 g / Energy: 525 kcal
Macronutrient ratio: Calories from carbs (6%), protein (29%), fat (65%)

Lamb Korma

Gentle, warming, and wonderfully creamy, this mild Indian curry will soothe and satisfy body and soul alike. If you have leftovers, so much the better: curries always taste best the day after they're made, because the flavors will have had time to combine.

Ingredients

2.65 pounds (1.2 kg) boneless leg of lamb
Salt and pepper
¼ cup (55 g/1.9 oz) ghee or other healthy cooking fat (see page 14), divided
1 medium (110 g/3.9 oz) yellow onion, chopped
1 recipe Korma Curry Paste (page 24)
1 cup (240 ml) bone broth (page 44) or vegetable stock (page 28)
1 whole star anise
Optional: pinch of saffron for yellow color
1 can (400 ml/13.5 fl oz) coconut milk
Suggested side: cauli-rice (page 18) or shirataki rice (page 19)
Fresh cilantro for garnish

Instructions

Preheat the slow cooker. Cut the lamb into 1½-inch (4-cm) chunks, and season with salt and pepper. To brown the lamb, grease a large heavy-based saucepan or Dutch oven with half of the ghee. Cook the lamb in batches until browned on all sides and transfer to the slow cooker.

Grease the pan where you cooked the lamb with the remaining ghee. Add the onion and cook over medium-high heat for 5 to 8 minutes, until lightly browned. Add the prepared Korma curry paste and cook for a minute, stirring frequently. Mix in the bone broth, star anise, and optionally a pinch of saffron. Transfer to the slow cooker and cover with a lid. Cook on low for 8 hours or on high for 4 hours. Stir in the coconut milk in the last 30 minutes of the cooking process. When done, discard the star anise, taste, and season if needed. Serve with steamed cauli-rice or shirataki rice. Garnish with fresh cilantro. To store, let it cool, and refrigerate for up to 4 days or freeze for up to 3 months.

NUTRITION FACTS PER SERVING (WITHOUT THE SUGGESTED SIDE):
Total carbs: 6.9 g / Fiber: 2.2 g / Net carbs: 4.7 g / Protein: 30 g / Fat: 45.3 g / Energy: 550 kcal
Macronutrient ratio: Calories from carbs (3%), protein (22%), fat (75%)

Irish Lamb Shanks

Traditional Irish stew is a simple yet delicious dish, but you can take it to the next level by using a couple of tricks: browning the meat before slow-cooking enhances the flavors, while adding the vegetables at the end of the cooking process makes them perfectly tender, but not mushy.

Ingredients

BOUQUET GARNI:

2 to 3 sprigs thyme
2 to 3 sprigs parsley
1 sprig rosemary
2 bay leaves

STEW:

4 small (1.4 kg/3 lb) bone-in lamb shanks, will yield about 50% meat
½ teaspoon fine sea salt, or to taste
Ground black pepper
2 tablespoons (30 g/1.1 oz) ghee or other healthy cooking fat (see page 14), divided
1 medium (110 g/3.9 oz) yellow onion, chopped
2 large (128 g/4.5 oz) celery stalks, sliced
1 cup (240 ml) bone broth (page 44) or water
10.6 ounces (300 g) green beans, trimmed and halved
8.8 ounces (250 g) baby turnips, halved, or 1 regular turnip, diced
Fresh parsley for garnish

Instructions

Preheat your slow cooker. Make the bouquet garni by placing all the herbs in a piece of cheesecloth and tying with unwaxed kitchen string. This will make it easy to remove once cooked.

Season the lamb shanks with salt and pepper. To brown the lamb, grease a large heavy-based saucepan or Dutch oven with half of the ghee. Cook the lamb over high heat in batches until browned on all sides and transfer to the slow cooker.

Grease the pan with the remaining ghee. Add the onion and cook over medium-high heat for 5 to 8 minutes, until lightly browned. Add the celery and cook for a minute. Add the bone broth and bring to a boil while scraping the browned bits off the bottom. Pour into the slow cooker and cook on low for 8 hours.

After 6 hours of cooking, using tongs, transfer the lamb to a plate. Place the green beans and turnips in the slow cooker and add back the lamb. Cook for another 2 hours, or until the green beans are crisp-tender and the meat is soft and juicy. Discard the bouquet garni and garnish with fresh parsley before serving. To store, let it cool, and refrigerate for up to 4 days. To freeze, first shred the meat off the bone and freeze for up to 3 months.

NUTRITION FACTS PER SERVING:
Total carbs: 12.7 g / Fiber: 4.2 g / Net carbs: 8.5 g / Protein: 32.6 g / Fat: 44.4 g / Energy: 583 kcal
Macronutrient ratio: Calories from carbs (6%), protein (23%), fat (71%)

Chapter 6

DESSERTS

Slow cookers are great for making convenient no-fuss
soups, stews, and casseroles. But what if slow cooking
is not limited to savory soups and stews? By using a few
simple tricks, you can make anything from crunchy granola
and roasted nuts to creamy custard and even cheesecake!
All of the following recipes can be made in a slow cooker.

Spiced Orange Pudding

If you've got a handful of basic ingredients and a few minutes to spare, it's easy to whip up this elegant, creamy citrus pudding. Topped with homemade, sugar-free cranberry sauce, it makes a great dinner-party dessert.

Ingredients

- 1½ cups (360 ml) coconut milk or heavy whipping cream
- 5 egg yolks
- ¼ cup (40 g/1.4 oz) powdered erythritol or Swerve
- 1 tablespoon (6 g/0.2 oz) freshly grated orange zest or ½ teaspoon sugar-free orange extract
- ¼ teaspoon ground cinnamon
- ¼ teaspoon vanilla powder or 1 teaspoon sugar-free vanilla extract
- Pinch of salt
- Optional: 4 tablespoons (60 g/ 2.1 oz) Cranberry Sauce (page 43) on top (1 tablespoon per each custard)

Instructions

Preheat the slow cooker. Fill it with 1 cup (240 ml) of boiling water. Place a spacer inside the slow cooker (see page 12). Combine all the ingredients except the cranberry sauce, if using, in a bowl using a whisk. Pour the mixture into 4 ramekins and place them on top of the spacer. Cover the slow cooker with a lid and cook on low for 2 to 3 hours, until the custard is set. Remove the lid and let the custards cool to room temperature. Cover each ramekin with plastic wrap. Refrigerate for at least 2 hours or overnight. Once chilled, optionally top each one with a tablespoon (15 g/0.5 oz) of Cranberry Sauce (page 43).

NUTRITION FACTS PER SERVING:
Total carbs: 4.2 g / Fiber: 0.3 g / Net carbs: 3.9 g / Protein: 5.1 g / Fat: 23.7 g / Energy: 240 kcal
Macronutrient ratio: Calories from carbs (6%), protein (8%), fat (86%)

Carrot Cake Oatmeal

Feel like having dessert for breakfast? (Of course you do. Who doesn't?) Perk up your morning with this filling, grain-free oatmeal made with nuts, coconut, carrots, pumpkin, and warming autumn spices.

Ingredients

¼ cup (55 g/1.9 oz) virgin coconut oil

2 cups (480 ml) unsweetened almond milk or cashew milk

1 cup (240 ml) coconut milk

½ cup (100 g/3.5 oz) unsweetened pumpkin purée (page 26)

⅓ cup (83 g/2.9 oz) almond butter or coconut butter

½ cup (38 g/1.3 oz) unsweetened shredded coconut

1 cup (110 g/3.9 oz) grated carrot

½ cup (58 g/2 oz) chopped walnuts or pecans

3 tablespoons (30 g/1.1 oz) granulated erythritol or Swerve

1 teaspoon fresh lemon or orange zest

½ teaspoon vanilla powder or 2 teaspoons sugar-free vanilla extract

1 tablespoon (8 g/0.3 oz) pumpkin pie spice (or make your own, page 22)

¼ cup (38 g/1.3 oz) chia seeds

Optional: few drops of liquid stevia

OPTIONAL TOPPINGS:

Creamed coconut milk (see page 27), heavy whipping cream, or mascarpone cheese

Toasted flaked almonds or coconut

Roughly chopped pecan or walnut pieces

Instructions

Preheat the slow cooker. Place all the ingredients apart from the chia seeds in the slow cooker, and heat through for about 1 hour. When the mixture is warm, add the chia seeds and combine well. Cover with a lid and cook on low for 3 to 4 hours, stirring once or twice. When done, taste and add stevia if needed. Serve warm or cold with any optional toppings. To store, let it cool, and place in an airtight container. Store in the fridge for up to 5 days.

NUTRITION FACTS PER SERVING (¾ CUP/180 G/6.4 OZ):
Total carbs: 13.9 g / Fiber: 7.5 g / Net carbs: 6.4 g / Protein: 8.2 g / Fat: 34.3 g / Energy: 389 kcal
Macronutrient ratio: Calories from carbs (7%), protein (9%), fat (84%)

"Apple" Pie Crumble

There's nothing as comforting as the scent of a freshly baked apple pie on a cool fall evening, is there? With this low-carb version, which uses zucchini in place of apples, you can feel free to dig right in!

Ingredients

CRUMBLE TOPPING:

¼ cup (57 g/2 oz) butter or virgin coconut oil

2 cups (200 g/7.1 oz) almond flour

¼ cup (50 g/1.8 oz) granulated erythritol or Swerve

1 teaspoon ground cinnamon

"APPLE" PIE BASE:

6 (1.2 kg/2.6 lb) medium zucchini

¼ cup (57 g/2 oz) butter or virgin coconut oil

1 tablespoon (8 g/0.3 oz) ground cinnamon

1 teaspoon vanilla powder or 1 tablespoon (15 ml) sugar-free vanilla extract

1 teaspoon ground nutmeg

1 tablespoon cream of tartar

3 tablespoons (45 ml) fresh lemon juice

½ cup (100 g/3.5 oz) granulated erythritol or Swerve

Optional: few drops of liquid stevia

Optional: serve with mascarpone cheese, sour cream, whipped cream, or creamed coconut milk (see page 27)

Instructions

Preheat the slow cooker and add the butter to let it melt. To make the crumble topping, mix the almond flour, erythritol, and cinnamon. Add the butter, and use your hands to combine into a crumbly dough. Set aside.

Peel, halve, and quarter the zucchini lengthwise and cut the middle part off (use leftover zucchini cores to make Ratatouille Soup, page 59). Cut the zucchini into ½-inch (1-cm) thick slices and place them in the slow cooker. Add the butter, cinnamon, vanilla, nutmeg, cream of tartar, lemon juice, erythritol, and optional stevia. Using a spatula, combine the zucchini with all the spices, and then add the crumble topping. Place 2 layers of high-absorbent paper towels or a tea towel on top of the ceramic bowl and cover with a lid (see tips for reduced condensation, page 12). Cook on low for 2 to 3 hours, until the zucchini is tender. Serve with mascarpone cheese, sour cream, whipped cream, or creamed coconut milk. To store, place in an airtight container, and refrigerate for up to 5 days or freeze in manageable servings for up to 6 months.

NUTRITION FACTS PER SERVING:
Total carbs: 9 g / Fiber: 3.6 g / Net carbs: 5.4 g / Protein: 5.7 g / Fat: 20.1 g / Energy: 226 kcal
Macronutrient ratio: Calories from carbs (10%), protein (10%), fat (80%)

Snickerdoodle Crème Brûlée

If there's a single dessert in this world that's made for a slow cooker, it's got to be crème brûlée. This foolproof method results in evenly cooked, creamy custards with perfectly crispy tops.

Ingredients

- 2 cups (480 ml) coconut milk or heavy whipping cream
- 5 egg yolks
- ¼ cup (40 g/1.4 oz) powdered erythritol or Swerve, plus 4 teaspoons granulated erythritol or Swerve for topping
- 1 teaspoon ground cinnamon
- ½ teaspoon vanilla powder or 2 teaspoons sugar-free vanilla extract
- Pinch of salt

Instructions

Preheat the slow cooker and fill it with 1 cup (240 ml) of boiling water. Place a spacer inside the slow cooker (see page 12). Combine all the ingredients, apart from the 4 teaspoons of erythritol, in a bowl using a whisk. Pour the mixture into 4 ramekins and place them on top of the spacer, cover the slow cooker with a lid, and cook on low for 2 to 3 hours, until the custard is set. Remove the lid and let the custards cool to room temperature. Cover each ramekin with plastic wrap. Refrigerate for at least 2 hours or overnight.

When ready to serve, sprinkle each one with a teaspoon of granulated erythritol or Swerve (see tip below). Place under a broiler set to high for 3 to 5 minutes to caramelize, or use a blowtorch.

TIP: You can use Swerve to make the caramelized topping. Although erythritol will create a hard shell, it will not brown. Swerve contains fructooligosaccharides, which will help the tops brown and create the sugar effect.

NUTRITION FACTS PER SERVING:
Total carbs: 5 g / Fiber: 0.3 g / Net carbs: 4.7 g / Protein: 5.7 g / Fat: 29.8 g / Energy: 295 kcal
Macronutrient ratio: Calories from carbs (6%), protein (7%), fat (87%)

Pumpkin Pie Custard

The best part of pumpkin pie is the smooth, spiced, spoonable filling, so I came up with this no-fuss keto version of everyone's favorite fall treat. Like the Snickerdoodle Crème Brûlée on page 181, making it in your slow cooker results in the ideal texture—no guesswork required.

Ingredients

CUSTARDS:

1 cup (240 ml) coconut milk or heavy whipping cream

1 cup (200 g/7.1 oz) unsweetened pumpkin purée (make your own, page 26)

2 large eggs

¼ cup (40 g/1.4 oz) powdered erythritol or Swerve

1 teaspoon pumpkin pie spice (make your own, page 22)

½ teaspoon vanilla powder or 2 teaspoons unsweetened vanilla extract

Pinch of salt

TOPPING:

½ cup (120 g/4.2 oz) creamed coconut milk or mascarpone cheese

2 tablespoons (30 ml) liquid coconut milk or heavy whipping cream

¼ teaspoon ground cinnamon

Optional: few drops of liquid stevia

Instructions

Preheat the slow cooker. Fill it with 1 cup (240 ml) of boiling water. Place a spacer inside the slow cooker (see page 12). Combine all the custard ingredients in a bowl using a whisk. Pour the mixture into 4 ramekins and place the ramekins on top of the spacer. Cover the slow cooker with a lid and cook on low for 2 to 3 hours, until the custard is set. Remove the lid and let the custards cool to room temperature. Cover each ramekin with plastic wrap. Refrigerate for at least 2 hours or overnight.

To make the topping, combine the creamed coconut milk, liquid coconut milk, cinnamon, and optionally a few drops of stevia. When the custards are chilled, top each one with a dollop of the prepared topping.

NUTRITION FACTS PER SERVING:
Total carbs: 8.9 g / Fiber: 2.4 g / Net carbs: 6.5 g / Protein: 6 g / Fat: 25 g / Energy: 268 kcal
Macronutrient ratio: Calories from carbs (9%), protein (9%), fat (82%)

MAKES: 16 servings (about 8 cups)
PREPARATION TIME: 10 minutes
COOKING TIME: 3 to 4 hours

Spiced Bacon Granola

Bacon goes with absolutely everything, and that includes this nutty, crunchy, grain-free breakfast granola. The bacon lends it a savory twist, but it's also lightly sweet and super-satisfying.

Ingredients

6 slices (180 g/6.4 oz) unsmoked bacon

½ cup (120 ml) water

2 tablespoons (30 g/1.1 oz) extra-virgin coconut oil

¼ cup (63 g/2.2 oz) almond butter or coconut butter

1½ cups (90 g/3.2 oz) unsweetened coconut flakes

¾ cup (56 g/2 oz) unsweetened shredded coconut

1 cup (140 g/5 oz) whole almonds, roughly chopped

1 cup (100 g/3.5 oz) pecan or walnut halves, roughly chopped

½ cup (65 g/2.3 oz) pumpkin seeds or sunflower seeds

2 tablespoons (16 g/0.6 oz) chia seeds or flax seeds

1 tablespoon (8 g/0.3 oz) ground cinnamon

1 teaspoon vanilla powder or 1 tablespoon (15 ml) sugar-free vanilla extract

¼ cup (50 g/1.8 oz) granulated erythritol or Swerve (can be skipped)

Suggestions: serve with unsweetened nut milk (page 27), coconut milk, or yogurt

Instructions

Preheat the slow cooker. Place the bacon pieces in a large pan and add the water. Cook over medium-high heat until the water starts to boil. Reduce the heat to medium and cook until the water evaporates and the bacon fat is rendered. Reduce the heat to low and cook until the bacon is lightly browned and crispy. Set aside.

Place the coconut oil and almond butter in the slow cooker and let it melt. In a bowl, mix the coconut flakes, shredded coconut, almond and pecan pieces, pumpkin seeds, chia seeds, cinnamon, vanilla, and erythritol. Place all the ingredients, including the crisped-up bacon and bacon grease, in the slow cooker, and combine using a spatula. Cover with a lid and cook on low for 3 to 4 hours, mixing every hour to prevent burning. When done, let the granola cool, and then transfer to a jar. Store at room temperature for up to 1 month. Serve with coconut milk, almond milk, or full-fat yogurt.

NUTRITION FACTS PER SERVING (½ CUP/40 G/1.4 OZ):
Total carbs: 7.1 g / Fiber: 4.5 g / Net carbs: 2.6 g / Protein: 7.2 g / Fat: 21.6 g / Energy: 244 kcal
Macronutrient ratio: Calories from carbs (4%), protein (13%), fat (83%)

Spiced Macadamia Nuts

These slow-cooker-roasted macadamias are insanely delicious, and what's more, they're so good for you, because they're high in heart-healthy fats and low in carbs. Just do your best to stick to the recommended serving size: once you start eating them, it's hard to stop!

Ingredients

- 4 cups (540 g/1.2 lb) macadamia nuts
- 2 tablespoons (27 g/1 oz) virgin coconut oil, melted
- ¼ cup (40 g/1.4 oz) brown sugar substitute such as Sukrin, or erythritol, or Swerve
- ½ teaspoon ground cinnamon
- ½ teaspoon vanilla powder or 2 teaspoons sugar-free vanilla extract
- ½ teaspoon fine sea salt

Instructions

Preheat the slow cooker and line it with heavy-duty parchment paper. This will help the nuts cook evenly without burning. Place the macadamia nuts, melted coconut oil, and all the remaining ingredients into the slow cooker. Use a spatula to combine until the nuts are coated in the spices and oil on all sides. Cover with a lid and cook for 2 hours, mixing every 30 minutes to prevent burning. When done, remove the lid and let them cool. Transfer to a jar or an airtight container. Store at room temperature for up to 1 month.

NUTRITION FACTS PER SERVING (¼ CUP/35 G/1.2 OZ):
Total carbs: 4.8 g / Fiber: 2.9 g / Net carbs: 1.9 g / Protein: 2.7 g / Fat: 27.3 g / Energy: 258 kcal
Macronutrient ratio: Calories from carbs (3%), protein (4%), fat (93%)

Chocolate Chip Cookie Bites

Need to make a big batch of cookies in a matter of minutes? No problem! This recipe for keto cookies couldn't be easier, and the result is a perfectly bite-size treat that's delicious with a dollop of whipped cream, coconut cream, or yogurt.

Ingredients

2 cups (500 g/1.1 lb) almond butter or nut butter of choice

1 cup (250 g/8.8 oz) coconut butter, or more nut butter

2 large eggs

2 egg yolks

½ cup (100 g/3.5 oz) granulated erythritol or Swerve

½ teaspoon fine sea salt

1 tablespoon freshly grated lemon or orange zest

1 teaspoon vanilla powder or ground cinnamon

2 teaspoons gluten-free baking powder

1 cup (100 g/3.5 oz) pecan or walnut halves, chopped

3.5 ounces (100 g) dark chocolate chips or chopped chocolate bar (minimum 85% cacao)

Suggested topping: whipped cream or creamed coconut milk

Instructions

Line the slow cooker with heavy-duty parchment paper (see tips for reduced condensation, page 12). Preheat the cooker to low.

Place the almond butter, coconut butter, eggs, egg yolks, erythritol, salt, lemon zest, vanilla, and baking powder in a food processor. Pulse for a few seconds until well combined. Transfer the dough to the slow cooker and add the pecan halves and chocolate chips, pressing them into the dough and spreading the dough evenly. Cover and cook for 2 to 3 hours on low, flipping the bowl halfway through to ensure even cooking.

When done, turn the slow cooker off and remove the lid. Let it sit in the slow cooker for at least 2 hours. Cut into 20 pieces, and let the cookie bites cool completely. Instead of slicing, you can simply spoon a serving (about 65 g/2.3 oz) of cookie crumbles into a bowl and serve with whipped cream or creamed coconut milk. Transfer to a container. Store uncovered at room temperature for up to 1 week, or freeze for up to 6 months.

NUTRITION FACTS PER SERVING:
Total carbs: 9.9 g / Fiber: 5.7 g / Net carbs: 4.2 g / Protein: 7.7 g / Fat: 25.9 g / Energy: 311 kcal
Macronutrient ratio: Calories from carbs (6%), protein (11%), fat (83%)

Lemon Drizzle Cake

Looking for a summery, tangy, guilt-free dessert? This no-starch citrus cake is the answer: it's my low-carb take on English celebrity chef Mary Berry's legendary lemon drizzle cake.

Ingredients

CAKE:

2 cups (200 g/7.1 oz) almond flour

⅓ cup (40 g/1.4 oz) coconut flour

½ cup (100 g/3.5 oz) granulated erythritol or Swerve

¼ cup (25 g/0.9 oz) unflavored or vanilla whey protein powder or egg white protein powder

2 teaspoons gluten-free baking powder

½ teaspoon vanilla bean powder or 2 teaspoons sugar-free vanilla extract

½ cup (120 ml) almond milk, at room temperature

½ cup (114 g/4 oz) butter or coconut oil, melted

6 large eggs, at room temperature

Zest of 2 lemons (about 2 tablespoons or 12 g)

Optional: few drops of stevia

LEMON DRIZZLE TOPPING:

¼ cup (50 g/1.8 oz) granulated erythritol or Swerve

¼ cup (60 ml) hot water

Juice from 2 lemons (about 60 ml/½ cup)

1 tablespoon (10 g/0.4 oz) powdered erythritol or Swerve, for dusting

Instructions

Line the slow cooker with heavy-duty parchment paper (see tips for reduced condensation, page 12). Preheat the cooker to low. In a bowl, mix all the dry ingredients for the cake: almond flour, coconut flour, erythritol, protein powder, baking powder, and vanilla powder. In a mixer, process the almond milk, melted butter, eggs, lemon zest, and optionally a few drops of stevia. Slowly sift the prepared dry mixture into the wet mixture until well combined.

Pour the dough in the slow cooker. Cover, and cook on low for 2 to 3 hours. When done, remove the lid and let the cake cool for a few minutes.

Prepare the lemon drizzle. Dissolve the erythritol in a small saucepan with the hot water, and then add the lemon juice. Use the back of a spoon and drizzle it over the cake. Let it sit for 1 to 2 hours. Grab the parchment paper to remove the cake from the slow cooker. Use a fine-mesh sieve to sprinkle the powdered erythritol over the cake and slice it (see page 13 for tips). Keep at room temperature for up to 3 days, or freeze for up to 6 months.

NUTRITION FACTS PER SERVING:
Total carbs: 5.6 g / Fiber: 2.2 g / Net carbs: 3.4 g / Protein: 8.7 g / Fat: 18 g / Energy: 212 kcal
Macronutrient ratio: Calories from carbs (6%), protein (17%), fat (77%)

Spiced Chocolate & Coconut Cake

This cake is based on a Czech cake called pernik. Its unique mixture of warming spices makes it very special, and while it's usually baked in the oven, I think its texture actually improves when it's prepared in a slow cooker.

Ingredients

PERNIK SPICE MIX:

2 tablespoons (16 g/0.6 oz) ground cinnamon

1 tablespoon (5 g/0.2 oz) ground ginger

1½ teaspoons ground cloves

1½ teaspoons ground allspice

1 teaspoon ground coriander

½ teaspoon star anise powder

½ teaspoon vanilla powder

¼ teaspoon ground cardamom

¼ teaspoon ground nutmeg

¼ teaspoon fennel seeds

⅛ teaspoon cayenne pepper

CAKE:

1 cup (120 g/4.2 oz) coconut flour

1¼ cups (100 g/3.5 oz) ground walnuts, pecans, or sunflower seeds

¾ cup (150 g/5.3 oz) granulated erythritol or Swerve

½ cup (43 g/1.5 oz) cacao powder

1 tablespoon (7 g/0.3 oz) gelatin powder

1 tablespoon (12 g/0.4 oz) gluten-free baking powder

Instructions

Line the slow cooker with heavy-duty parchment paper (see tips for reduced condensation, page 12). Preheat the cooker to low. Prepare the spice mix by combining all the ingredients. (Store the leftover spice mix in an airtight container.)

In a bowl, mix all the dry ingredients for the cake: coconut flour, ground walnuts, erythritol, cacao powder, gelatin, baking powder, and 1 tablespoon plus 1 teaspoon (13 g/0.5 oz) of the prepared spice mix. In a mixer, process the coconut milk, melted butter, eggs, lemon zest, and optionally a few drops of stevia. Slowly sift in the prepared dry mixture until well combined.

Transfer the dough to the slow cooker and spread it evenly with a spatula. Cover and cook on low for 2 to 3 hours, until set. When done, remove the lid and let the cake cool for several hours.

Prepare the topping. Break the chocolate into pieces and place in a bowl with the spice mix. Heat the cream and butter over medium heat. When hot, pour over the chocolate. Mix until smooth and creamy. Pour on top of the cake, sprinkle with the shredded coconut, and let it sit for 1 to 2 hours. Grab the parchment paper to remove the cake from the slow cooker and slice (see page 13 for tips). Place in an airtight container. Refrigerate for up to 5 days, or freeze for up to 6 months. Any leftover pernik spice mix should be stored in an airtight container for up to a year.

Nutrition facts per serving:
Total carbs: 11.5 g / Fiber: 5.3 g / Net carbs: 6.2 g / Protein: 9.4 g / Fat: 28.2 g / Energy: 325 kcal
Macronutrient ratio: Calories from carbs (8%), protein (12%), fat (80%)

1 tablespoon plus 1 teaspoon
   (13 g/0.5 oz) pernik spice mix
1 cup (240 ml) coconut milk,
   at room temperature
½ cup (114 g/4 oz) butter or
   coconut oil, melted
6 large eggs, at room temperature
1 tablespoon (6 g/0.2 oz) freshly
   grated lemon or orange zest, or
   1 teaspoon sugar-free lemon or
   orange extract
Optional: few drops of liquid
   stevia

TOPPING:
3.5 ounces (100 g) dark chocolate
   (minimum 85% cacao)
½ teaspoon pernik spice mix
¼ cup plus 2 tablespoons (90 ml)
   coconut milk or heavy whipping
   cream
3 tablespoons (43 g/1.5 oz)
   butter or coconut oil
1 cup (75 g/2.7 oz) unsweetened
   shredded coconut

MAKES: 13 servings
PREPARATION TIME: 10 minutes
COOKING TIME: 2 to 3 hours + chilling

Macadamia Chai Cake

If your go-to coffee shop treat is a chai tea latte, you'll adore this gently spiced quick-prep slow cooker cake. It's incredibly nutritious, too, because it's packed with macadamias, which are high in B vitamins and minerals like iron, magnesium, and manganese.

Ingredients

CHAI SPICE MIX:

½ **teaspoon vanilla powder**
½ **teaspoon ground cinnamon**
½ **teaspoon ground nutmeg**
½ **teaspoon ground cloves**
½ **teaspoon ground cardamom**
½ **teaspoon ground allspice**
¼ **teaspoon ginger powder**
¼ **teaspoon fennel seeds**

CAKE:

¾ **cup (188 g/6.6 oz) coconut butter (a.k.a. coconut manna)**
1 **cup (134 g/4.7 oz) macadamia nuts**
½ **cup (100 g/3.5 oz) granulated erythritol, Swerve, or brown sugar substitute such as Sukrin**
1 **cup (240 ml) coconut milk, at room temperature**
4 **large eggs**
2 **teaspoons gluten-free baking powder**
Pinch of fine sea salt
Optional: few drops of liquid stevia

Instructions

Line the slow cooker with heavy-duty parchment paper (see tips for reduced condensation, page 12). Preheat the cooker to low. Prepare the spice mix by mixing all the ingredients.

Place the coconut butter and macadamias in a food processor, and process until smooth. Add the erythritol, coconut milk, eggs, baking powder, salt, and optionally a few drops of stevia. Process for a few seconds until well combined.

Transfer the dough to the slow cooker. Cover, and cook on low for 2 to 3 hours. When done, remove the lid and let the cake cool. Grab the parchment paper to remove it from the slow cooker and slice (see page 13 for tips). Keep at room temperature for up to 3 days, or freeze for up to 6 months.

NUTRITION FACTS PER SERVING:
Total carbs: 6.3 g / Fiber: 3.4 g / Net carbs: 2.9 g / Protein: 4 g / Fat: 21 g / Energy: 217 kcal
Macronutrient ratio: Calories from carbs (5%), protein (7%), fat (88%)

MAKES: 13 servings
PREPARATION TIME: 20 minutes
COOKING TIME: 2 to 3 hours + chilling

Chocolate Hazelnut Cake

Nutella, the famous chocolate-hazelnut spread adored by kids and grown-ups alike, is packed with sugar, so you'll need to avoid it if you follow a keto or low-carb lifestyle. But the good news is that you can enjoy its sweet-and-nutty taste in this simple, sugar-free chocolate cake.

Ingredients

CAKE:

2 cups (200 g/7.1 oz) almond flour

1⅓ cups (100 g/3.5 oz) ground peeled hazelnuts (see tip below)

¾ cup (150 g/5.3 oz) granulated erythritol or Swerve

½ cup (43 g/1.5 oz) cacao powder

1 teaspoon vanilla bean powder or 1 tablespoon sugar-free vanilla extract

2 teaspoons gluten-free baking powder

1 cup (240 ml) almond or hazelnut milk, at room temperature

½ cup (114 g/4 oz) butter or coconut oil, melted

4 large eggs, at room temperature

Optional: few drops of liquid stevia

Instructions

Line the slow cooker with heavy-duty parchment paper (see tips for reduced condensation, page 12). Preheat the cooker to low. In a bowl, mix all the dry ingredients for the cake: almond flour, ground hazelnuts (see tip on how to peel them before grinding), erythritol, cacao powder, vanilla, and baking powder. In a mixer, process the almond milk, melted butter, eggs, and optionally a few drops of stevia. Slowly sift the prepared dry mixture into the wet mixture until well combined.

Pour the batter into the slow cooker. Cover, and cook on low for 2 to 3 hours. When done, remove the lid and let the cake cool.

Prepare the topping. Break the chocolate into small pieces and place in a bowl with the vanilla. Heat the cream and butter over medium heat. When hot, pour over the chocolate. Mix until smooth and creamy. Pour on top of the cake, sprinkle with the roasted hazelnuts, and let it sit for 1 to 2 hours. Grab the parchment paper to remove the cake from the slow cooker and slice (see page 13 for tips). To store, place in an airtight container. Refrigerate for up to 5 days or freeze for up to 6 months.

TIP: To roast and peel hazelnuts: Preheat the oven to 375°F (190°C, or gas mark 5). Spread the hazelnuts on a baking sheet. Place in the oven and bake for about 10 minutes. Remove from the oven and cool for 15 minutes. Rub the hazelnuts in your hands to remove the skins (these would taste bitter). Grind them into a fine powder in a food processor.

Nutrition facts per serving:
Total carbs: 10.8 g / Fiber: 4.9 g / Net carbs: 5.9 g / Protein: 9.5 g / Fat: 35 g / Energy: 371 kcal
Macronutrient ratio: Calories from carbs (6%), protein (10%), fat (84%)

3.5 ounces (100 g) dark chocolate
(minimum 85% cacao)

½ teaspoon vanilla bean powder
or 2 teaspoons sugar-free
vanilla extract

¼ cup plus 2 tablespoons (90 ml)
coconut milk or heavy whipping
cream

3 tablespoons (43 g/1.5 oz)
butter or coconut oil

1 cup (115 g/4.1 oz) chopped
roasted hazelnuts

Brownie Almond Cheesecake Bars

This luscious keto treat is the perfect marriage of two popular desserts—almond cheesecake and dark, fudgy chocolate brownies—and you won't believe they're actually sugar-free. Serve with a hot cup of coffee or tea.

Ingredients

CHEESECAKE LAYER:

1 cup (240 g/8.5 oz) full-fat cream cheese, at room temperature

¼ cup (58 g/2 oz) full-fat sour cream

½ cup (125 g/4.4 oz) almond butter, softened

1 egg yolk

1 large egg

¼ cup (40 g/1.4 oz) powdered erythritol or Swerve

½ teaspoon ground cinnamon

1 teaspoon sugar-free almond extract

Optional: few drops of liquid stevia

BROWNIE LAYER:

3.5 ounces (100 g) dark chocolate (minimum 85% cacao)

4.4 ounces (125 g) butter or coconut oil, melted

3 large eggs

¾ cup (120 g/4.2 oz) powdered erythritol or Swerve

1 cup (100 g/3.5 oz) almond flour

½ cup (43 g/1.5 oz) cacao powder

¼ cup (32 g/1.1 oz) ground chia seeds

2 teaspoons gluten-free baking powder

¼ teaspoon fine sea salt

Instructions

Line the slow cooker with heavy-duty parchment paper (see tips for reduced condensation, page 12). Preheat the cooker to low. Place all the cheesecake ingredients in a mixing bowl: cream cheese, sour cream, softened almond butter, egg yolk, egg, erythritol, cinnamon, almond extract, and optionally a few drops of stevia. Set aside.

To prepare the brownie layer, break the chocolate into pieces and add to a heatproof bowl with the butter. Place over a pan filled with simmering water and make sure the water doesn't touch the bowl: only the steam should heat the bowl. Slowly melt while stirring. When most of the chocolate is melted, remove the pan from the burner and let the mixture continue to melt. Set aside.

Place the eggs and powdered erythritol in another bowl and whisk until well combined. Beat in the chocolate mixture and gently fold in the almond flour, cacao powder, ground chia seeds, baking powder, and salt, and process well.

Pour the brownie batter into the slow cooker and spread evenly. Top with the prepared cheesecake mixture. Cover and cook on low for 3 to 4 hours. When done, remove the lid and let cool. Once cooled, grab the parchment paper to remove the cake from the slow cooker, and slice (see page 13 for tips). To store, place in an airtight container. Refrigerate for up to 5 days or freeze for up to 6 months.

NUTRITION FACTS PER SERVING:
Total carbs: 10 g / Fiber: 4.6 g / Net carbs: 5.4 g / Protein: 9 g / Fat: 29.3 g / Energy: 323 kcal
Macronutrient ratio: Calories from carbs (7%), protein (11%), fat (82%)

New York Cheesecake with Chocolate Ganache

This classic deli-style dessert is rich, creamy, satisfying—and, of course, completely starch-free. And it's so simple: "baking" the cake in your slow cooker yields a perfectly creamy texture each and every time.

Ingredients

CRUST:

1 cup (100 g/3.5 oz) almond flour

2 tablespoons (28 g/1 oz) butter or virgin coconut oil

¼ cup (40 g/1.4 oz) powdered erythritol or Swerve

1 egg yolk

½ teaspoon vanilla bean powder or ground cinnamon

Pinch of fine sea salt

CHEESECAKE LAYER:

2 cups (480 g/16.9 oz) full-fat cream cheese, at room temperature

½ cup (114 g/4 oz) full-fat sour cream

1 egg yolk

1 large egg

½ cup (80 g/2.8 oz) powdered erythritol or Swerve

½ teaspoon vanilla bean powder or 2 teaspoons sugar-free vanilla extract

2 tablespoons (30 ml) fresh lemon juice

1 teaspoon fresh lemon zest

Instructions

Preheat a 5- to 6-quart (4.7- to 5.7-L) slow cooker and fill with 1 cup (240 ml) of boiling water. Place a spacer inside the slow cooker (see page 12). Line the bottom of a medium springform pan with parchment paper. Make sure the springform pan fits in the slow cooker and the bottom doesn't touch the water.

Combine all the ingredients for the crust: almond flour, butter, erythritol, egg yolk, vanilla, and salt. Mix using your hands and press into the bottom of the springform pan. Set aside while you prepare the cheesecake layer.

In a bowl, using a whisk or an electric mixer, mix the cream cheese, sour cream, egg yolk, egg, erythritol, vanilla, lemon juice, lemon zest, and coconut flour. Optionally, add a few drops of stevia. Pour into the springform pan over the almond crust.

Place the springform pan in the slow cooker on top of the spacer. Cover, and cook on low for 4 hours. When done, turn off the heat, remove the lid, and let cool. Leave the cheesecake in the slow cooker to cool for 2 to 3 hours. Refrigerate in the springform pan overnight. When ready to make the chocolate ganache, gently remove the cheesecake from the springform pan by running the side of a blunt knife between the edge of the cheesecake and the pan.

Prepare the chocolate ganache. Break the chocolate into small pieces and place in a bowl with the vanilla. Heat the cream and butter over medium heat and, when hot, pour over

NUTRITION FACTS PER SERVING:
Total carbs: 6.9 g / Fiber: 1.8 g / Net carbs: 5.1 g / Protein: 7.6 g / Fat: 29.3 g / Energy: 295 kcal
Macronutrient ratio: Calories from carbs (6%), protein (10%), fat (84%)

1 heaped tablespoon
   (12 g/0.4 oz) coconut flour
Optional: few drops of liquid
   stevia

GANACHE:

3.5 ounces (100 g) dark chocolate
   (minimum 85% cacao)
½ teaspoon vanilla bean powder
   or 2 teaspoons sugar-free
   vanilla extract
¼ cup plus 2 tablespoons (90 ml)
   heavy whipping cream or
   coconut milk
3 tablespoons (43 g/1.5 oz)
   butter or coconut oil
Optional: few drops of liquid
   stevia

the chocolate. Mix until smooth and creamy. Leave to cool slightly, and then pour over the cheesecake. Let it chill in the fridge for at least 10 minutes before slicing. Store in an airtight container in the fridge for up to 5 days or freeze for up to 6 months.

TIP: Don't panic if the ganache separates. You can fix it by placing it in a blender or a food processor with 1 to 2 tablespoons (15 to 30 ml) of hot water. Process until smooth and creamy.

Index

About the Author

Martina Slajerova is a health and food blogger living in the United Kingdom. She holds a degree in economics and worked in auditing, but has always been passionate about nutrition and healthy living. Martina loves food, science, photography, and creating new recipes. She is a firm believer in low-carb living and regular exercise. As a science geek, she bases her views on valid research and has firsthand experience of what it means to be on a low-carb diet. Both are reflected on her blog, in her KetoDiet apps, and in this book.

The KetoDiet is an ongoing project she started with her partner in 2012 and includes *The KetoDiet Cookbook*, *Sweet and Savory Fat Bombs*, *Quick Keto Meals in 30 Minutes or Less*, and the KetoDiet apps for the iPad and iPhone (www.ketodietapp.com). When creating recipes, she doesn't focus on just the carb content: You won't find any processed foods, unhealthy vegetable oils, or artificial sweeteners in her recipes.

This book and the KetoDiet apps are for people who follow a healthy low-carb lifestyle. Martina's mission is to help you reach your goals, whether it's your dream weight or simply eating healthy food. You can find even more low-carb recipes, diet plans, and information about the keto diet on her blog: www.ketodietapp.com/blog.

Acknowledgments

I'd like to thank everyone at Fair Winds Press who put so much hard work into my new cookbook. Special thanks to Jill Alexander, Renae Haines, Heather Godin, Lydia Finn, Jenna Patton, and Megan Buckley.